I0714445

Art's Properties

ART'S PROPERTIES

DAVID JOSELIT

Princeton University Press

Princeton and Oxford

Library of Congress Cataloging-in-Publication Data

Names: Joselit, David, author.
Title: Art's properties / David Joselit.
Description: Princeton : Princeton University Press, [2023] |
Includes bibliographical references and index.
Identifiers: LCCN 2022005105 (print) | LCCN 2022005106 (ebook) |
ISBN 9780691236049 (hardback) | ISBN 9780691236056 (ebook)
Subjects: LCSH: Art—Philosophy.
Classification: LCC N66 .J67 2023 (print) | LCC N66 (ebook) |
DDC 701—dc23/eng/20220720
LC record available at https://lccn.loc.gov/2022005105
LC ebook record available at https://lccn.loc.gov/2022005106

British Library Cataloging-in-Publication Data is available

Book design by Monograph / Matt Avery

This book has been composed in Lyon Regular No. 2, Mint Grotesk, and Mint Book

Printed on acid-free paper. ∞

Printed in the United States of America

1 3 5 7 9 10 8 6 4 2

for my students

Contents

I don't know why I don't just send all my desire forward.
BENJAMIN KRUSLING

Prologue

Museums are photo opportunities. Rather than merely housing art, they *generate* images: their galleries function as stage sets for the auto-performance of selfies, and their exhibitions furnish archives from which spectators select and capture artworks in cell-phone snaps. They facilitate a mode of production, in which pictures lead to more pictures to be stored in personal collections that need not conform to authoritative art histories. Some museums have even begun to adjust their design to accommodate this mode of production. Depot Boijmans Van Beuningen in Rotterdam, which opened in 2021, literally turns the museum on its head by consolidating its storage into an open archive displayed in a freestanding bowl-shaped structure with a mirrored facade. As the institution's website explains: "Depot Boijmans Van Beuningen is the first depot in the world that offers access to a complete collection. The dynamics of the depot are different from that of the museum: no exhibitions are organized here, but you can—independently or with a guide—browse through

151,000 art objects" (fig. 1).[1] The distinction between a *museum* (which shapes its presentations as exhibitions) and a *depot* (which offers access to a complete collection or archive) is crucial here. Unlike a museum, the depot delegates its curatorial responsibility to individual visitors, who may "browse" either "independently or with a guide." Even the building's exterior offers a photo opportunity. Like the reflective 2004 sculpture *Cloud Gate* by Anish Kapoor in Chicago's downtown Millennium Park, which is a favored backdrop for selfies, the Depot Boijmans Van Beuningen will inevitably become a virtual landmark. The depot is the logical terminal point in an emergent architectural typology—the museum as strongbox. This was the concept of the Schaulager in Basel, founded in 2003, whose name is itself a combination of the German words for "show" (*Schau*) and "warehouse" (*Läger*). The Broad Museum in Los Angeles, which like the Schaulager is built around a private collection, is similarly conceived. As the website recounts:

> Dubbed "the veil and the vault," the museum's design merges the two key components of the building: public exhibition space and collection storage. Rather than relegate the storage to secondary status, the "vault" plays a key role in shaping the museum experience from entry to exit. Its heavy opaque mass is always in view, hovering midway in the building. Its carved underside shapes the lobby below, while its top surface is the floor plate of the exhibition space. The vault stores the portions of the collection not on display in the gal-

leries or on loan, but [architects] DS+R provided viewing windows so visitors can get a sense of the intensive depth of the collection and peer right into the storage holding.[2]

What this typology of open or visible storage acknowledges spatially—and ideologically—is that museums have begun to function as brick-and-mortar search engines, where each human spectator behaves like an embodied algorithm, a curatorial agent of selection.

But how does an algorithm see? Machine vision, in which no human agent intervenes, emerges when an artificial intelligence program is "trained" to recognize images through the analysis of large archives. The artist Trevor Paglen has explored the aesthetics of machine vision, while scholars like Safiya Umoja Noble and Ruha Benjamin have demonstrated the implicit biases that result when computers are trained on image archives saturated with sexist and racist representations.[3] The human algorithm, equipped with a camera and cruising a museum (or depot), would seem to have greater autonomy than a mathematical procedure. But, in fact, visitors are often drawn to a small number of iconic images that have become famous in part because they have often been photographed before. In 2017 the Broad Museum ("the veil and the vault") found it necessary to impose a thirty-second time limit inside each of Yayoi Kusama's installations, to ease their patrons' wait times. As one visitor complained, "I got a little stressed because you had like one second to take pictures."[4] Such an imperative to photograph reorganizes contemplation. Time is no longer spent in looking, but in waiting; seeing takes place in a flash, through a camera, affording just enough time to expose an image. It is easy to discount such assembly-line spectatorship as peripheral to the museum's mission—or conversely as a sign of its thorough commodification—and to condemn selfies in particular as narcissistic. Few people find it pleasant to approach artworks framed by a ring of glowing screens grasped in museumgoers' raised hands. And yet, the collapse of seeing into photographing, which has occurred in museum galleries around the world, is worth taking seriously as a distinctive practice of spectatorship. It consists of two moments: *capture*, in which the artwork is *taken* as a photo; and *curation*, wherein the spectator-photographer arranges pictures for their own pleasure or to post on social media. The rhythm of capture and curation elides contemplation in what might be called the *possessive gaze*. This gaze is possessive in at least two ways. First, it is *self-possessive*, in that it documents a viewer's presence before the artwork in a selfie. And second, through the capture and curation of images, the viewer appropriates the museum's procedures of aesthetic judgment—by acquiring art (*capturing it*) and exhibiting it (*curation*). Spectatorship is repositioned: the museumgoer is no longer merely a consumer of the museum's authoritative narrative, but rather she regards its displays as the raw material for her own second-order curatorial agency. She claims sovereignty, then, not just over her own body and individual

artworks but over the museum's narrative. Her possessive gaze competes with that of the museum.

Certainly, not everyone who visits museums or galleries looks through a camera. And yet, the scene of
photography in museums exemplifies a broader condition of possessive modes of looking. These motivate
museum labels (which tell people what to see, capturing
the artwork in a "discursive snapshot") or the popular
fascination with art markets and fairs (in which optical
experience is elided with a price that affords artists their
"market snapshot"). Paradoxically, then, the possessive
gaze is founded on a constituent act of dispossession:
the dispossession of artworks as singular, generative
experiences. In the nearly instantaneous cell-phone
transaction of capture and curation, the scanning of a
long label, or the preoccupation with art's economic
value, art's material specificity is all but foreclosed,
along with its proffer of durational experience. "I got a
little stressed because you had like one second to take
pictures," said the visitor to the Broad in 2017. The possessive gaze is premised on art's alienability through
images, as a kind of derivative currency.[5] In a way, one
might even regard it as a reaction to the extreme dispossession of human sight in the face of machine vision. The embodied algorithm wants to reclaim itself
as central to the act of seeing, and yet it often defaults
to something like machine vision. In 1936 Walter Benjamin argued that such procedures of mechanical reproduction robbed artworks of their material specificity—
what he called their *aura*.[6] Nearly one hundred years

later, another reading is possible. The auratic mystique of the artwork is not diminished but doubly *deferred* for future use—as a kind of credit. It is literally placed in storage in the memory of electronic devices to be consulted later or put into circulation as a form of cultural capital through its distribution on social media. Most significantly, the temporal *experience* of the artwork is deferred: instead of looking, the museumgoer is storing and sharing his experience in a handheld digital "depot." If we think of artworks as durational artifacts (ranging from moving images with a literal duration to paintings or photographs that invite contemplation of an unspecified period of time), the museum presents a sublime temporal challenge. Who, after all, can really exhaust the vast experiential offerings of even a modest-sized exhibition? Indeed, it was said of curator Okwui Enwezor's *documenta 11* exhibition in 2002 that there was "more time-based work than could be seen by a single person in the one hundred days that the exhibition was open."[7] The conundrum here is that artworks cannot, in fact, be consumed. Yes, they can be bought and sold, or transformed into digital images and circulated. But the nature of a work of art lies in its experiential inexhaustibility. Whether one wants it or not, it will keep on giving. It is this infinite temporality that is given finitude by the possessive gaze. The spectator's relationship to the museum is one of building credit: credit for future experience. I imagine museumgoers lamenting, as Benjamin Krusling does in the beautiful line that serves as my epigraph, "I don't know why I don't just send all my desire forward." The museum is a strongbox not only of valuable objects but of unimaginable durations, more time than can ever be spent, and yet, the possessive gaze cannot be dissuaded from trying to store it up.

If, as many experts agree, Western economies should now be considered "experience economies," where value is inherently durational, the capture of artworks as digital images is a form of conspicuous consumption in reverse—a hoarding of deferred experience, as "experiential credit." From individual households to high-rolling hedge funds, finance is structurally dependent on accruing credit as a means of survival for some and speculation for others. Under these conditions, the museumgoer's practices of photography may be considered a form of neoliberal performance art, enacting and re-enacting the primal scene of credit building as deferred experience. But what exactly is being deferred? How might we characterize the temporality of art that lures museumgoers into rituals of capture? In looking, one's attention may play freely across different passages or segments of a work, from different distances, and at varying speeds. The gaze may be caught momentarily by a vigorous painterly passage, or made to stutter in a randomized video loop or pause in horror at the photograph of a battlefield. The possibilities are limitless, but what all artworks share is the composition of durations. In such scenes of looking, as opposed to the possessive gaze of capture and curation, the gaze is dispossessed, literally ecstatic in its unregulated capacity for free play.

If we think of artworks as temporal compositions—or scores—which may be played differently by different spectators in any single instance, then we have a model of visual art as a durational medium.[8] Such temporal scores evoke a kind of dispossession that everyone is familiar with from everyday experience: if you meet a friend in a restaurant and suddenly realize, as a server brings your drinks, that this is the same bistro where you fought with an ex-lover six years ago, you will find yourself occupying two moments at once, being two different people at once, while remaining in the same place—having a pleasant drink and reliving a wrenching breakup. This is a simple experiential score—you could play it as a performance of sullen silence toward your friend or as a way of building intimacy with her by telling the story of your soured relationship. If the anecdote I just recounted were published in textual form as a memoir, then an additional layer of complexity is introduced by all successive readers, each of whom would have played the score of their reading as the singular experience of their own personal associations and projections. What visual art offers is the *spatialization* of such different affective responses, set side by side so that their harmonies and contradictions may become visible. Works of art score a complex configuration of durations, played differently by each spectator, each time they look. The wild sensation of freedom that artworks may inspire is not political in a conventional sense of the term, simply because the time of the artwork is radically different from the everyday negotiations and struggles that constitute conventional politics. Artworks compose a vertiginous cocktail of futurity in their expectation to live on through time, or the evidence of their already having done so, while nonetheless proffering an experience of absolute presentness. The freedom I will identify within works of art is the freedom to at once occupy the here and now, and an "elsewhere" or "otherwise," which in the course of *Art's Properties*, I will define as art's constituent alterity.

In his definitive history of the discipline of art history, Christopher S. Wood repeatedly returns to a striking paradox. He argues that, as "distinguished from other artifacts by the multiplicity of its origin points both within and beyond historical time," art *cannot be captured by history*. The discipline of art history is something like a reaction formation: it promises the history of something whose ontological qualities ensure that it escapes historicization. "Modern art history," Wood says, "is obliged to carry on delivering knowledge, knowledge about a kind of non-knowledge." Wood's diagnosis is emphatic: "Art history that really keeps pace, and faith, with art cannot be a history anymore."[9] This declaration returns us to the museumgoer as photographer. Unlike the feckless art historian, who, despite their erudition and assiduity, can never *capture* an artwork as an art-historical document, the museumgoer with a cell phone hopes to circumvent this difficulty by locking art into a digital form that may be stored—by passing the artwork forward into the future as a form of experiential credit. Each proceeds from the same desire—the desire to possess art's temporal freedom. This desire is real, and it has existed through time, though the terms and conditions of its experiential proffer, and the attempts by various powers to capture it, have always been historically specific. The politics of art have little to do with art's participation in current events (for which it is not well suited) and much to do with its power to summon alterity, an "elsewhere" or "otherwise." The politics of art is the story of that alterity's capture, whether by art historians, the Christian church, absolute monarchs, twenty-first-century oligarchs, or the authors of selfies in contemporary museums. *Art's Properties* will narrate scenes from the emergence and capture of modern art, and it will recommend a solution to the double bind described by Wood. If art cannot be captured by history, it may nonetheless generate unlimited narratives. In this regard, the museumgoer-photographer again demonstrates something fundamental: if the value of art can never be captured, nor can it be fully consumed. The power of art is its capacity—its *infinite* capacity—to generate experience over time.

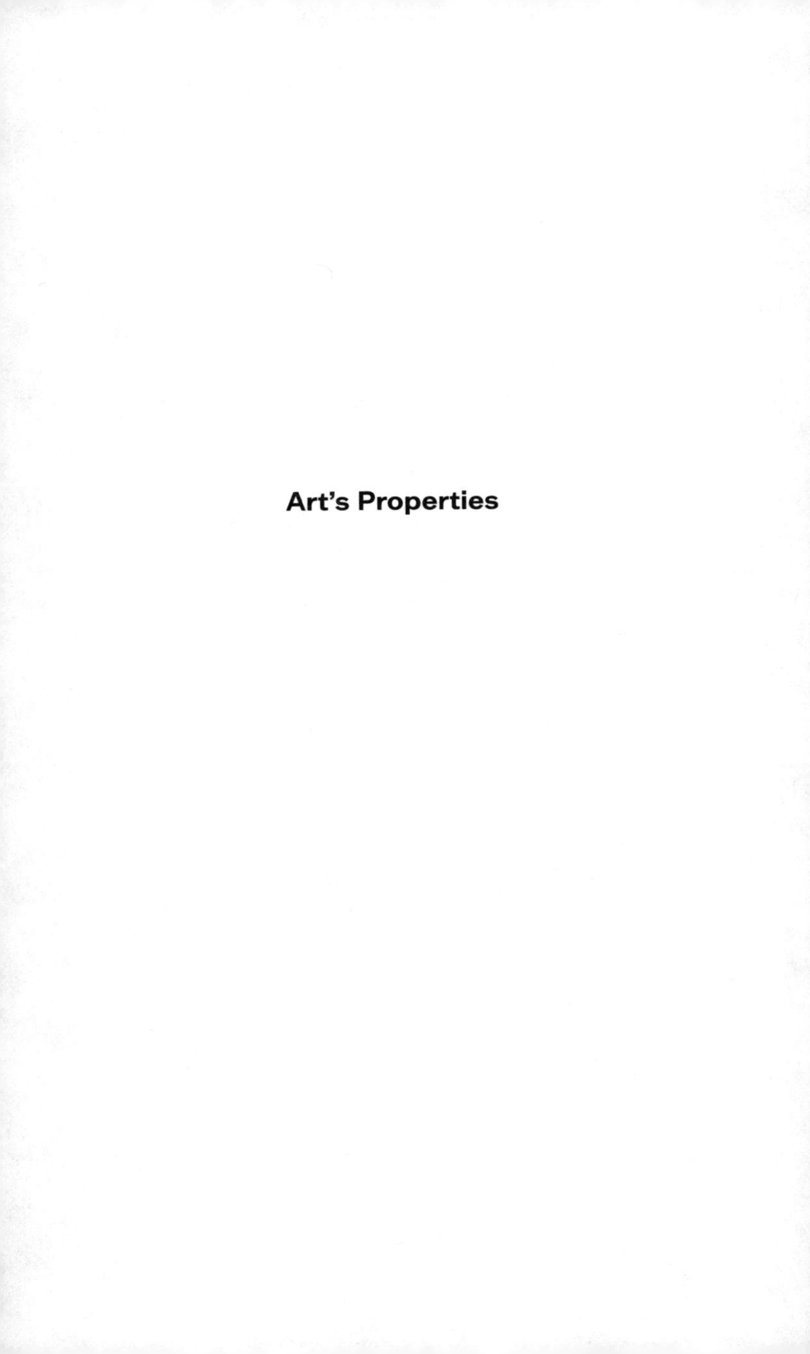

Art's Properties

Alienability and Alterity

When museumgoers turn to cell phones, their possessive gaze renders artworks alienable by transforming them into digital images. This is one of the several ways in which modern and contemporary art is subject to circulation virtually and physically. It is transposed into information and consumed as knowledge (in formats ranging from extended labels displayed on museum walls to art-historical monographs), and it is sold as commodities whose value is specified by a price. But this dynamic of alienability goes far beyond individual works of art to encompass a vast chain of proprietary relationships that establish the identity and territoriality of cultures. Artworks are regarded as the intellectual property of their authors and, in turn, the cultural property of whatever nation, community, or identity these authors are assigned to. In all cases, alienability is enabled through acts of representation: a digital photograph represents the experience of an artwork; interpretive discourse represents the artwork as a quantum of meaning or a historical document; the auctioned artwork represents a market value; intellectual property represents the legal limits of an artist's creativity; and cultural property represents a nation, class, gender, or ethnicity. As a procedure of capture and curation, representation and exchange work hand in hand. Think, for instance, of paper currency, which, unlike precious metals such as silver or gold, has no intrinsic value but merely *represents* value. Paper money accomplishes a strategic impoverishment—in order to enable exchange, it must attenuate its own materiality. So it is with art: when artworks are represented by a reproduction, an interpretation, a price, an author, or an identity, they are alienated as a currency of experience, knowledge, or value. The cost of such transpositions is significant. By sublimating the artwork's materiality, such chains of representation falsify its ontological fundament: its experiential inexhaustibility over time. The artwork's duration is curtailed, transposed into finite exchangeable properties.

Nonetheless, the power of art remains the durational infinitude it stages. It straddles the here and now and an elsewhere or otherwise. It is an opening to various forms of alterity whose capture has been, throughout history, a source of worldly power. What is Christ? An alterity whose susceptibility to representation has been tested through time in paint, wood, plaster, and stone. What is absolutism? An alterity that the *premier peintre du roi* Charles Le Brun brought to bear upon the body of Louis XIV at Versailles. What is revolution? Consider Soviet artists Varvara Stepanova and Lyubov Popova, who investigated the intimacy of revolutionary alterity through redesigning the furnishings of everyday life. The history of art is drawn from such socially embedded performances of alterity—each iteration activates singular effects of power that range from consolidating despotism to challenging white supremacy. The temporality of these effects is distinct from the rhythms of conventional politics. Alterity's elsewhere or otherwise does not take place in the exclusively human realm of the state, or civil society. Art's special capacity is to configure multiple registers of experience (the spiritual, the terrestrial, the abstract, and the material) rather than remaining embroiled in the ephemeral conflicts of day-to-day politics. Its power *is its capacity to activate alterities*. This capacity has always been coveted because the colonization of alterity through its representation can realize or legitimize power—it can assist someone in becoming a pope or becoming an absolutist king or becoming the avant-garde. But because art's alterity lies in its infinite and heterogeneous duration, it can never be thoroughly objectified or commodified; it can only be alienated in new derivatives, never exhausted. These derivatives are produced through acts of representation in which art's duration is fixed in a single transactional moment of representation where one thing is made to stand in for another.

In distinguishing the infinite and hetereogenous temporality of artworks from historical time, characterized by the organization of successive choronological periods, Henri Focillon wrote, in 1934:

The artist inhabits a country in time that is by no means necessarily the history of his own time. He may ... be thoroughly contemporary with his age and may even, because of this fact, adapt himself to the artistic activities going on around him. With equal consistency he may select examples and models from the past, and create from them a new and complete environment. He may, again, outline a future that simultaneously strikes into the present and the past. But a sudden shift in the equilibrium of his ethnic values may bring him into violent opposition with his environment and hence with the moment, and arouse a nostalgia in him that is highly revolutionary.[1]

"A *country* in time" does not denote a *period*, which is defined by a span of contiguous years. Countries in time are more like topographies composed of geological strata whose sedimented layers, each indexing a different era, are reorganized by tectonic or volcanic pressure, pushing one stratum through another, or allowing them to fall back on one another. According to Focillon, such quasi-geological temporal formations may become revolutionary: "a sudden shift in the equilibrium of [an artist's] ethnic values may bring him into violent opposition with his environment and hence with the moment, and arouse a nostalgia in him that is highly revolutionary." This association of nostalgia with revolution is the antithesis of avant-garde orthodoxy: unlike the latter it rejects a linear progression in time, but like it, it defines revolution as a temporal rupture.[2] That this rupture is accounted for by "a sudden shift in … ethnic values" is a mark of how time and identity can exist in a state of mutual destabilization—a kind of parallax that, in fact, makes it incoherent to force an artist to represent a period or an ethnicity, as she is often made to do in art-historical accounts.

In telling time, the clock *represents* all forms of temporal experience with the same standardized abstract units. Art's duration, like that of the earth, escapes clock time and thus escapes history. Indeed, this is the further distinction Focillon draws with his geographic metaphor, of "a country in time that is by no means necessarily the history of *his own* time" (my italics). This declaration may seem an anodyne reference to the romantic or bohemian artist—one who is out of step with the norms of the time in which she lives. But Focillon means much more here—in fact, he accomplishes an elegant and subtle, though deadly serious, challenge to the discipline of art history. For, as I argued above, the significance and meaning assigned to artworks in most scholarship and criticism is premised on a possessive chain of representation that enables art to function as an alienable asset: creativity comes to represent the artist; the artist in turn represents national history and culture, while this heritage is used to represent a nation-state (and, moreover, each of these relations is reversible: the artist represents creativity; nation and culture represent an artist; and heritage is understood as national). I have italicized Focillon's possessive expression when he declares that the artist's country in time is not "necessarily the history of *his own* time," because even in Focillon's careful effort to distinguish between an artist and his era, the representational relation returns in the notion of one's *own* time. This is because the representational mechanism is fundamental not only to art history—in which the artist becomes a document of her time—but also to the value of art more generally. That which can be represented can be possessed (as image, knowledge, wealth, personal identity, or group identity). That which exceeds representation, which is outside the possessive gaze, is inalienable. The mark of this disruption for Focillon is "a sudden shift in the equilibrium of [an artist's] ethnic values." In other words, the artist ceases to represent an ethnicity and thus becomes other to herself.

What Focillon theorizes is art's alterity vis-à-vis the possessive gaze; following his analysis, artists cannot be made to represent "their" time because they inhabit a different "country in time." Moreover, an artist's alterity to herself (what Focillon describes as a potential disruption of her "ethnic equilibrium") disqualifies her to represent a finite identity—indeed to force her into such a mold is to commit a kind of conceptual violence. It is the argument of *Art's Properties* that the power of art lies in such excess or alterity—in its capacity to elude capture. But despite art's recalcitrance (or perhaps on account of it), its excess accrues power through the desire for sacred and secular authorities to channel it as a mode of worldly legitimacy. The politics of art inheres less, then, in art itself than in various gambits to harness its force as a means of authorization. As Marie-José Mondzain declares, with regard to the economy of representation constructed around Byzantine icons: "Christian discourse, taken as a whole, is nothing other than an immense ordering and management of the question of the image, whether it is flesh, sin, women, nature, or art that are concerned."[3] The ordering that Mondzain traces is different from the possessive gaze of modernity; it is the gaze of God filtered through various incarnations (of Christ as the image of his Father, and the icon as the image of Christ, hence the image of an image): "It could be said that what the icon imitates is not the vision that humans cast at things but God's imagined gaze that is cast upon humans."[4] While icons were circulated widely, their authoritative gaze was wholly centralized, whereas in modern times the possessive gaze is not located in a chain of images whose ultimate source is God but atomized as the *private* properties of everyone, susceptible to exchange. Regardless of this enormous and significant difference between Byzantium and modern Euro-America, the desire to capture alterity as a form of worldly power has persisted through time. Indeed, it has persisted *as* time— that is, art's opening to alterity lies in its capacity to assemble and compose diverse experiences of duration. The artwork is a composition of time, a kind of attentional score, or what Mondzain might call an economy of the gaze. In the case of the icon, the Christian god represents a powerful form of alterity to be captured: its temporal signature is eternity. In our time, as I have already argued, art has tended toward an economy of instantaneous exchange, a stock market of cultural capital that has most recently resulted in rampant speculation in NFTs, or non-fungible tokens—"unique" digital properties whose aesthetic value, and even de facto rarity, is often nominal, but whose market value as art has nevertheless exploded.

In order to grasp the particular violence involved in making art alienable, it is crucial to understand its ontological resistance to capture. For despite assumptions to the contrary, artworks are dedicated not to representation but to its *failure*. This is because every work of art has two bodies, a material substrate with its own mortality, and an image or series of images characterized by immortality.[5] Unlike the letters that compose words—like the ones you are reading now—whose efficacy is based on their transparency to an intended meaning, the material that constitutes an artwork's substrate always offers an excess—an optical and affective richness that is ultimately impossible to capture in its singularity. In its very structure, the artwork itself is an allegory of capture—the capture of an image by matter. But such capture is impossible to achieve. Sometimes it is the image that shines through with minimal interference, but frequently it is a material substrate that dominates, as in nonobjective painting, where there may be no recognizable image beyond the formal disposition of matter.

In other words, every work of art testifies to the paradoxical impossibility of representation—its material and conceptual precarity—because no work can achieve perfect transparency of its substrate to its image. It would not be art if it did. Matter, whether oil paint or a digital file, is both subject to time, in that it has a life span, and a principle of time's organization, in that its aesthetic texture may score the spectator's gaze. The mortality of matter is abundantly evident if one takes the time to notice it. The varnish on old master paintings turns yellow or brown; certain pigments are unstable; photographs fade; wooden objects may become infested with insects; film has been known to burst into flames; in video's short life as an art medium, its standards have changed several times; even, or especially, digital art is not immune to accelerating cycles of technical obsolescence. The work of art requires enormous care in order to survive intact—whole cadres of preparators, registrars and conservators are required to maintain a museum's investment in art's persistence through time as self-identical. Each material experiences its own temporality of decay and recovery and undergoes its own sedimentation in time. Each work also has a specific play of textures, its own aesthetic means of capturing attention. Moreover, these material temporalities may undermine the meaning or authority of a work, as when a photograph, believed to accomplish the instantaneous capture of an actual scene, is also subject to evanescence through fading—a vulnerability that, on account of museum standards requiring lower light levels and limited exposure for works on paper, conditions how and when a photograph will be publicly displayed.

The image or images to which an artwork's material substrate is linked are of an entirely different ontological (and temporal) order from that of matter. I will follow Jean-Paul Sartre in defining an image as a psychic effect—as a *relation* between a spectator, in whose consciousness the image appears, and a material substrate that is the occasion, or pretext, for its appearance. The image isn't *in* the work of art—it is brought to it by each spectator (including the artist, as the initial spectator) through their intention. Consequently, it is ephemeral and unstable—even more so because the function of the image is to posit an absent object: "The image is an act that aims in its corporeality at the absent or nonexistent object, through a physical or psychic content that is given not as itself but in the capacity of an 'analogical *representative*' of the object aimed at."[6] It is worth pausing to note how strange this entity—the image—is, despite its ostensible familiarity and ordinariness. As a psychic effect, it has no empirical body (it is independent from its material substrate). In principle, it is difficult if not impossible to verify that the image I receive from a particular painting, or photograph or film, is the image *you* see. In this sense, defining the image as a relation, as Sartre does, has significant social consequences. For, if we are to relate to one another through the medium of images, we must find some way to agree on what they are—or at least to accept a shared agonistic space for debate over their meaning. Right away, this definition suggests that the intending action of an image is characterized by three temporal signatures: instantaneity (its immediate appearance in the mind of the spectator); intermittence (as the function of a relation that may be broken or lost, its appearance is precarious); and displacement (in that the image makes present something that is physically absent). In an observation that highlights art's paradoxical combination of material and virtual constituents, Sartre draws a further important distinction between the image as an instantaneous form of consciousness and perception as a kind of knowledge gradually built up over time by accruing and combining sensory data. "In perception," he says, "knowledge is formed slowly; in the image, knowledge is immediate."[7] This distinction between gradual perception, which is how one encounters an artwork's substrate, and immediate image consciousness, characteristic of what it pictures, points to the constitutive failure of representation within the artwork. We encounter a material object through our sense organs, accruing different data over time in order to build an impression of it in our mind, while the image is recognized in the material substrate instantaneously. Sartre himself points to the crossing of perception and intention as fundamental to the experience of art: "the painting should be conceived as a material thing *visited* from time to time (every time the spectator takes the imaging attitude) by an irreality that is precisely the *painted object*."[8] As I have suggested in my discussion of the material temporalities of art's substrates, the painting "as a material thing" may also inspire a panoply of images beyond those intended by the artist—what we may call the vicissitudes of the material itself, or its unconscious. But perhaps even more important, attending closely to the materiality of the work can cause one to lose track of the intended image. Far from being the scene of transparent representation, the artwork is a trap for the image—a gambit for building social relations that may, as I have demonstrated, become a consequential medium of worldly power.

Throughout art's history, its ontological alterity—its constitutive self-difference as a composition of divergent temporalities generated through the unstable alliance of matter and image—served to embody various kinds of alterity. Mondzain's analysis of icons offers just one example of a vast category of art's incarnation of alterity: its capacity to make divine beings manifest and thus subject them to human manipulation and desire. As I have already indicated, in modernity, the precarious, unstable relation of image and matter and the complex and contradictory temporalities it generates are disciplined into a form of representation—a kind of currency—in which the inalienable multiplicity and fecundity of an artwork is pressed into alienable forms of property. But as in Byzantium, where the alterity of art was tied to the alterity of the Christian god, in modern times there is a specific form of difference that art is privileged to carry: nation, ethnicity, race, and personal markers of identity such as gender and sexuality. While this dynamic may seem contemporary, in the next section I will demonstrate that already with the invention of the first democratic museum—the Louvre—a complex modern regime was established, in which a new form of power—first revolutionary and then, with Napoleon, imperial—was devised, wherein authority was amassed as the accumulation of cultural properties, as embodied in art.

Constituent Moments
1793–1815

The Louvre is often claimed to be the first democratic museum. What is less frequently acknowledged is that its invention depended upon both the nationalization of artworks within France and their seizure as trophies of war from foreign nations. From the start, the modern museum crystallized a politics of art's alienability. Twenty-first-century struggles over the repatriation of artworks within Europe and between Europe and the Global South focus primarily on the return of cultural properties taken by settler colonialists or looted as spoils in punitive colonial military expeditions. Such works entered museums not only through violent means but also in explicit efforts to annihilate the cultural sovereignty of colonized people through the destruction of their religions, customs, and aesthetic practices. One cruelly ironic justification for the seizure of cultural property by Euro-American museums—that these appropriations are a means of salvaging dying cultures (or, in its more recent form, that Western museums are technically better equipped to care for objects from the Global South)—is that the very Western "protectors" who claim to save this patrimony were those who looted it in the first place! Some of the most passionate and theoretically interesting contemporary debates about art—and particularly the politics of art—pertain to questions of restitution. Demands for repatriation are ethically complex and go to the heart of what it means to "possess" culture, to make it one's own or one's community's property. The stakes of these debates are those that animate *Art's Properties*: if not all cultural properties are alienable—that is, not legitimately subject to individual ownership or exchange—then on what grounds should art be considered inalienable? By what rights does one claim possession or moral rights over a particular work, image, or subject matter? As we will see, the assertion of moral rights over certain forms of cultural property is by no means restricted to struggles between the Global North and South. Indeed, alongside contemporary struggles over cultural restitution have been fierce debates over who is authorized to represent whom in contemporary works of art in Europe and North America—a struggle that is often misleadingly associated with a return of 1990s forms of identity politics.

Given how urgent questions of cultural property are in the third decade of the twenty-first century, one might be forgiven for believing that these debates originated with the unfinished project of decolonization, in which the formal political dismantling of colonial states has led to demands for more thoroughgoing ideological transformations, including the decolonization of museums. But in fact, as the cultural policies of the French Revolution and First Empire demonstrate, the alienability of artworks—and struggles around the legitimacy of their transfer—are the *constituent moments* of the modern museum. Conversely, we might claim that the modern museum enables the artwork's modern alienability. I draw the term *constituent moment* from the work of political theorist Jason Frank, who uses it to describe how "a people" was enacted as the grounds for claims of democratic sovereignty in the politics of the postcolonial United States. For Frank, *the people* can only be known through representation. But because this collectivity is not some empirically available or pre-given entity (don't forget that enslaved African Americans, as well as women and noncitizens of all ethnicities, are examples of groups that once were or still are excluded from this category in the United States), the people can *only* be established through representation. The problem with representation in this context is that despite its utility for democracy, it is simultaneously *anti-democratic*, in that it inherently limits what the category of "the people" is or can be. Constituent moments, then, are moments of representation that betray the alterity that haunts democracy: "Constituent moments invent a new political space and make apparent a people that are productively never at one with themselves."[1] Two important consequences follow from this formulation: first, the form and materiality of "the people" is nothing more or less than a representation; and second, this representation is both enabling—in that it can make present the idea of a people—but also oppressive in that it limits those who are included in this category and how they will appear. Frank describes the paradox as follows: "The problem of the people enacted *through* representation but always escaping capture *by* representation is a formal dilemma of democratic legitimacy—the paradox of politics—and one that is continually renavigated not by logic or argument, but through competing narratives of collective belonging."[2]

The modern museum's constituent moment was coeval with the emergence of "the people" as a political agent in the French Revolution. One might say that the founding of the Louvre was a Declaration of the Rights of Man by other means. In the years between 1793 and 1815, two new institutions dependent upon an accelerated traffic in alienable cultural property were founded in France. In 1793 the Louvre opened as a public museum in conjunction with the festival of August 10, which, Andrew McClellan writes in *Inventing the Louvre*, "endorsed the reidentification of familiar Parisian landmarks as sites of Republican memory."[3] Both the festival and the museum were tools for representing something new: the sovereignty of the French people. As the painter and organizer of revolutionary events Jacques-Louis David recounted, with regard to the festival, "All individuals useful to society ... will be joined together as one; you will see the president of the executive committee in step with the blacksmith; the mayor with his sash beside the butcher or mason; the black African, who differs only in color next to the white European."[4]

Like other landmarks highlighted in the festival, the
Louvre also underwent a significant "reidentification"
from a princely collection to one dedicated to representing the liberty of the people. This included a peda-
gogically oriented shift in museology, from a model of
visual delectation to one of art-historical categorization,
which, as Isabelle Leroy-Jay Lemaistre outlines, was
consolidated by 1796:

> Museography was endlessly disrupted by the succes-
> sive and sometimes massive shipments of artworks;
> if in 1793 exhibitions of the King's paintings were ar-
> ranged solely based on their visual appeal, like a con-
> noisseur's gallery, by contrast, from 1796, following
> [Jacques-Louis] David's declarations on the exemplary
> value of art, these images could no longer be shown
> that way. In 1796 an exhibition at the Salon Carré of a
> portion of the King's paintings was organized accord-
> ing to [artistic] schools, numbered both on the picture
> rails and in the catalogues, allowing for the beginnings
> of a pedagogical discourse.[5]

Lemaistre makes clear that the reopening of the Louvre
eventually led to a genuine resignification of a collection that was dynamically growing—it was harnessed
as a pedagogical tool, a medium of representation that
could outline a history of the world through art that
would culminate in the French Revolution's celebration
of a global concept of liberty. This is undoubtedly why,
in the heat of revolution, so much attention was paid

to rapidly reorganizing and opening a new museum. Christopher Wood describes the apparent paradox this way: "It is hard to believe that in these weeks and months of turmoil, when state and nation were being ripped apart and stitched together again at the cost of thousands of lives, an art museum could achieve such significance."[6] It is less hard to believe when one recognizes that the Louvre's reorganization was a constituent moment in the representation of the French people. But the Louvre represented another important lesson, indicated by Lemaistre's reference to the perpetual growth of its collections, first on account of appropriated possessions of French churches and aristocrats and subsequently in Napoleon's numerous campaigns in Europe and Egypt, in which waging war converged with cultural appropriation. From one perspective, the nationalization of large amounts of art taken from aristocratic and church collections within France framed the reorganization of the Louvre as a massive act of restitution: a kind of repatriation of France's patrimony, seized from its secular and ecclesiastical elites and given to its people. For Napoleon, beginning with his revolutionary campaign in Belgium, where art was appropriated for France, and exemplified by his campaign in Italy at the end of the revolutionary period, which culminated in a triumphal procession of looted works in Paris in 1798, the Louvre became not only (or perhaps not anymore) the image of the people's sovereignty but also a monument to France's pretended status as the *representa-*

tive of Western civilization (fig. 2). Though he was not a connoisseur, Napoleon was highly alert to the power of art, and of the museum in particular, as a tool for asserting his legitimacy as emperor. His looting was organized, informed by expert opinion, and often legitimized by treaty. As Cecil Gould described it, the enormously powerful director of the Musée Napoléon (as the Louvre was renamed in 1803), Dominique Vivant Denon, "was quick to realize the basis of looting in time of war: regardless of whether or not a pseudo-legal justification is envisaged in the armistice agreement or peace treaty the act of taking possession should be carried out immediately. The person responsible should, if possible, arrive at the depôt of the works of art on the heels of the shock troops."[7] For Napoleon, his museum was a stage for the assertion of power: "In the Louvre, in the antiquities galleries, Napoleon received military delegates after his coronation on December 8, 1804.... In the Louvre, he married Marie-Louise in 1810."[8]

Whether the Louvre represented a shift in sovereignty, from ecclesiastical and secular elites to the French people, or a subsequent transfer of sovereignty from the people to their newly proclaimed emperor, temporarily immortalized in the Musée Napoléon, both power effects were achieved through the transfer of alienable cultural properties. The patrimony of France briefly shifted from the property of its monarchy and elites to "the people," while the patrimony of Europe was captured and exhibited in Paris in a dazzling and unprecedented accumulation of trophies as the epitome of Napoleon's imperial sovereignty. A second institution, the Musée des Monuments Français, presided over by Alexandre Lenoir and originating in one of the depots where the nationalized goods of churches and aristocrats had been stored, took a different tack—it narrated the history of France itself through its cultural properties. Lenoir's museography was dedicated to creating a new historical context for works that had recently been extracted—*alienated*—from their native surroundings. Their function as church furnishings, for instance—especially funerary monuments—was evacuated. These objects, after all, were being stored in a warehouse, literally without context. To make any sense of them required a new narrative, a new set of conceptual relationships that could replace those they had lost. Lenoir furnished exactly that by organizing his galleries chronologically and according to artistic school, in order to offer a history of France through objects. Since the documents that constituted this "history" had been previously spread across several sites and obviously not arranged chronologically, this curatorial strategy, as familiar as it seems to us today, was radically new. To enhance their narrative force, Lenoir's galleries were designed to be atmospheric and picturesque; they were meant to immerse the viewer in an affective experience. As Lenoir expressed it, he wished to give "each of these galleries the character and exact physiognomy of the century that it was to represent."[9] This phrase is illuminating in its emphasis on *representation*. Once alienated from their specific ecclesiastical functions, or their purely aesthetic disposition in aristocratic picture collections or cabinets, these works were charged with *representing* the "physiognomy" of their century. They were quite literally transformed from devotional objects, for instance, to portraits of an era. By all accounts, this effort was a great success; the eminent nineteenth-century French historian Jules Michelet, for instance, remembered his "emotion, still the same, and still so sharp … when as a young child I walked in and searched, ardent, curious, timid, from room to room, from era to era."[10] If the Louvre initially represented the people of France as an abstract sovereign in rightful possession of the museum's patrimony, and Napoleon subsequently used his museum to establish imperial France as the representative of European culture, the Musée des Monuments Français afforded what we might call an ethnic history of the French nation.

Napoleon's intentions in establishing the Musée Napoléon as a manifestation of his power were well understood by the European nations whose patrimony had been looted in order to fill its galleries. After his defeat at Waterloo in 1815, insistent demands for the return of cultural properties were issued from across the continent. Prussian troops and later British officers were dispatched to the Louvre to recover art; the victorious Duke of Wellington was engaged on behalf of these efforts,[11] and the sculptor Antonio Canova—a celebrity artist whose work was coveted by an international elite including the Bonapartes—was dispatched by Pope

Pius VII to recover as many works taken from Rome by Napoleon's forces as possible. Perhaps surprisingly, these efforts met significant resistance from both the restored French monarch, Louis XVIII, and the Musée Napoléon's powerful director, Denon. Ultimately, a significant proportion of the booty remained in France.[12] If these struggles over repatriation represent the realpolitik of post-Napoleonic restitution, its theory was afforded by A.-C. Quatremère de Quincy, the eminent French scholar and archaeologist. Quatremère saw clearly that the museum collections built during the revolution and empire were mechanisms for art's alienation—its transformation into a deracinated form of currency. For him, the work of art derived its power from *sentiment*—an ineffable affective quality—which was closely tied to its intended "purpose" (French, *destination*) in space and time and, especially, to the community of spectators for which it was made. He contrasted *sentiment* to arid forms of intellectualized critique, which valorized the rules of form and historical comparison. The museum to him was a space where artworks were both drained of meaning and accumulated so wantonly as to render impossible a personal encounter between viewer and artwork. For Quatremère, then, art's animating principle—sentiment—was lost in the disorder of the warehouse, as he wrote in 1815: "Stop telling us that works of art are stored in these warehouses. Yes, you have transported them there physically, but were you able to transport the full flock of tender, profound, melancholy, sublime, or touching sensations that surrounded them?"[13] The "body" of art could be displaced but not its soul. In a statement directly contradicting Lenoir's strategy of historicization in the Musée des Monuments Français, Quatremère argues that the museum kills history:

> Moving all the monuments, so as to gather up their dispersed fragments, methodically classify their debris and make of this grouping a lesson in modern chronology is for a living nation to become a dead nation; it is for the living to attend their own funeral; it is to murder Art to write its history; it is not to write the history of art but its epitaph.[14]

One of the virtues of revisiting Quatremère's text is its passionate assertion that, at the very moment of its birth, modern museology had already assumed the form of what Dan Hicks has called "the Brutish Museum."[15] For Hicks, the brutality of museums lies in their explicitly colonial project, their murder of a subject people's culture through museumification and the perpetuation of such violent appropriation through the ongoing exhibition of spoils. In 1955, 140 years after Quatremère published his critique of the museum, the theorist of Négritude, Aimé Césaire launched nearly identical charges in his *Discourse on Colonialism*. But instead of attending to the intra-European plunder that Quatremère declaimed, Césaire decried the museum's symbolic murder of Europe's colonial subjects. In commenting on the museum, he declares:

Europe would have done better to tolerate the non-European civilization at its side, leaving them alive, dynamic and prosperous, whole and not mutilated; that it would have been better to let them develop and fulfill themselves than to present for our admiration, duly labelled, their dead and scattered parts; that anyway, the museum by itself is nothing; that it means nothing, that it can say nothing, when smug self-satisfaction rots the eyes, when a secret contempt for others withers the heart, when racism, admitted or not, dries up sympathy.[16]

In a famous passage in the *Discourse*, Césaire makes an analogy between the genocide perpetrated by Hitler in Europe and colonial atrocities in Africa and elsewhere. He says, of the white European: "What he cannot forgive Hitler for is not *the crime* in itself, *the crime against man*, it is not *the humiliation of man as such*, it is the crime against the white man, the humiliation of the white man, and the fact that he applied to Europe colonialist procedures that had been reserved exclusively for the Arabs of Algeria, the 'coolies' of India and the 'ni—ers' of Africa."[17] We might say that the nineteenth-century history of the museum inverts the chronology of this analysis but maintains its structure. A technology for creating deracinated cultural properties was invented in the intra-European conflict that erupted out of the French Revolution, only to be turned outward decades later toward Europe's colonies.[18] In both directions, the symbolic violence of museumification is described as a form of *death*, but what exactly is meant by such charges of object-murder? For Quatremère it is the death of sentiment, which is tied to the habitus of a particular people or community. For Césaire it is something similar—what is murdered is the non-European civilization's liveliness, that which makes it "dynamic and prosperous." These living qualities accessed through affective connection (i.e., sentiment or vivacity) are the fundaments of what I have called art's alterity, or the spectator's durational encounter with an optical vibrancy that defies capture. The death of this liveliness is also the death of alterity as a dynamic relation. The living object becomes a dead thing when its capacity to generate multiple meanings is extinguished—when it is made into a fixed *representation* of, for instance, primitivism or barbarism. Césaire understood such transformations as central to how European colonizers asserted claims of sovereignty—as he concisely put it: "colonization = 'thingification.'"[19] In other words, colonization turned vibrant objects (both cultural artifacts and individual colonized subjects) into fixed things, which were experienced as dead because of the sustained efforts to foreclose their capacity to generate alterity. If colonization = thingification, then sovereignty arises from the capture and curation of things, and the museum emerges as a form of governance.[20] This is the modern museum's constituent moment as a form of governmentality and oppression rather than liberty; it attempts to turn the living alterity of art into a static—or dead—representation of difference. This is what Mahmood

Mamdani means when he writes of British colonialism, "the definition and management of difference was developed as the essence of governance."[21] The museum is a laboratory for governance as curation.

In his 2020 book *Neither Settler nor Native*, Mamdani argues that "Nationalism did not precede colonialism. Nor was colonialism the highest or final stage of making a nation. The two were co-constituent."[22] Here is a more comprehensive account of political modernity's constituent moments than those I have offered thus far. When the modern nation-state is constituted—when, in other words, a dominant ethnicity is made to *represent* the people as a whole, an excess—those excluded from the ethnic category of the nation must nevertheless be governed. Mamdani recognizes the violence of such conditions of modern nationalism, and he gives them a name, *ethnic cleansing*: "The violence of postcolonial modernity mirrors the violence of European modernity and colonial direct rule. Its principal manifestation is ethnic cleansing."[23] For Mamdani, the constituent moments of political modernity are quite simply moments of ethnic cleansing—not only do they define *the people* as a subset of the population of a state, but they actively exclude the resulting "excess." Taking the United States as a paradigmatic postcolonial example (and the model for later repressive regimes such as South African apartheid), Mamdani describes two distinct techniques that the US nation-state developed to govern two groups that were alienated from the nation while nonetheless subject to its sovereignty—enslaved Africans and Native Americans:

> Blacks have been a source of labor and Indians a source of land, resulting in different governance regimes. Blacks have been governed by a regime of white supremacy, the struggle against which has been incorporated into the American sense of self—a fact demonstrated by the comfort with which racists cite [Martin Luther] King and other icons of civil rights. Indians, by contrast have been governed by colonialism, which, if recognized, would destroy the American sense of self.[24]

This description exemplifies what Mamdani theorizes as the race-tribe system of colonial governance. The core principle of racial subjection is the establishment of hierarchy within the laws of a state—"a regime of white supremacy." The enslaved person, for instance, was legally powerless to exercise the rights of a citizen yet was often held responsible for breaking the law. On the other hand, the tribal solution involves the sequestration of the subject people on, for example, an Indian reservation, and establishes conditions of indirect rule—where Native sovereignty is formally acknowledged but practically undermined through the subject state's dependence on the colonial power. I invoke Mamdani's distinction to help us better understand the ideological differences between the two museum types I have discussed thus far. The "universal" museum, whose paradigm is the

Louvre (or Musée Napoléon), was premised on exhibiting multiple national cultures and historical epochs in an implicit hierarchy. The fact that the preponderance of nations initially subjected to these judgments were European, does not significantly undermine Mamdani's model of a racial (or ethnic) sorting, for indeed the objective was the same: an assertion of French superiority or sovereignty over the nations of Europe. The second model of the museum, the Musée des Monuments Français, tells the story of a single nation, which is consistent with Mamdani's "tribal" solution—in this case it was nationalized properties of the *ancien régime* that told the history of a recently moribund culture of monarchy and its aristocratic and ecclesiastical elites. As Mamdani argues of US museumification of Native communities, historicization is a way to neutralize living traditions: "Indian culture was to an extent preserved, but it was placed in a museum, where it could no longer meet the problems of the moment or evolve to meet those of the future."[25] Indeed, Saloni Mathur and Kavita Singh have argued that the national museum was a typical cultural institution in colonial states such as India.[26] Its purpose, like that of the Musée des Monuments Français, was to trace an ethnic or civilizational particularity, in contrast to the supposed universality of metropolitan collections like the Louvre or the British Museum. Of course, the Musée des Monuments Français was a national museum dedicated to exhibiting the culture of a colonizing power. But it was precisely the museum of a France—the France of the *ancien régime*—that the revolution had dismantled and thus wished to consign to history. It is not by chance that the Musée des Monuments Français quickly collapsed after the fall of Napoleon, while the Louvre has continued to thrive.[27] After all, with the restoration of the French monarchy and the return of émigré aristocrats, an "ethnic" account of the *ancien régime* became not only redundant but politically inflammatory. In its efforts to come back to life, the *ancien régime* could hardly tolerate, let alone sponsor, its own museumification.

The bifurcated museology I have described was invented to reorganize through curation the recently alienated aesthetic heritage of the *ancien régime*, and the European cultural property looted from across the continent, into powerful ideological statements. The Louvre and the Musée des Monuments Français thus became important sites for representing the legitimacy of France's "co-constituent moment" of nationalism and colonialism. These representations had different emphases: The so-called universal museum arranges the cultural properties of foreign nations (both colonial "possessions" and European rivals) in a hierarchical order that visualizes the sovereign claims of the French empire. The Musée des Monuments Français, on the other hand, constructed the narrative of a single nation by historicizing it. As I have argued, it may seem contradictory to find a national museum identified with an imperial power until we recall that the Musée des

Monuments Français was founded on the nationalized properties of the recently defunct monarchy and its aristocratic and ecclesiastical elites—an ethnic museum of the *ancien régime*, as it were. If the universal museum is aimed at integrating diverse international patrimonies into a hierarchical formation, the national museum emphasizes the particularity of a civilization—a particularity, as Mathur and Singh have argued with regard to colonial national museums, that disqualifies such institutions from claiming universality. It must be remembered that the foundation of both types of museums was premised on a massive program of art's alienation as property—both through the nationalization of French cultural patrimony and the systematic wartime seizure of foreign art as an integrated component of Napoleon's military campaigns. We thus encounter, in the modern museum's co-constituent moment, the same dynamic of *capture and curation* that we witnessed among individual museumgoers in the practice of taking cell-phone images in galleries, only writ large. It should be clear by now that not every act of capture and curation is the same—each instance of capture extracts value from the durational alterity of artworks in different ways. It is not surprising, then, that universal and national museums developed their own curatorial semantics aimed at harnessing the durational alterity of artworks—transforming living alterity into dead representations of difference (which is precisely, as we have seen, how sovereignty is claimed). The semantic model of the Musée des Monuments Français was chronological.[28] In sorting and displaying its collections according to the era of their production, Alexandre Lenoir made artworks serve as *representations* of the physiognomy of an epoch. The ontologically ungovernable durational experience of individual artworks was consequently disciplined into an evolutionary narrative of France. As natural a framework of organization as chronology appears to us, it nevertheless severely limits how we understand the meaning of individual artifacts—as *documents* or representations of an era. Though sections of the Musée Napoléon's collections were also arranged chronologically, or by artistic schools, its curatorial strategy depended more on a supplemental, ideologically significant temporal signature—that of allegory, which is characterized by the animation of a past moment in the present in order to claim the authority of cultural heritage on behalf of contemporary agents—in this case Napoleon. For instance, the classical sculptures that French troops had looted from Italy, which since the Renaissance had been closely identified with the power and glory of the Roman Empire as well as the highest form of European erudition, were arranged to suggest an analogy with Napoleon's own imperial pretensions—which, in the visual culture surrounding his reign, had been consistently saturated with the language of classicism. Bringing the past into the present through allegory was a form of power that Napoleon had borrowed from the *ancien régime* itself, where absolutist kings were often represented in the guise of gods (though such signification typically took place in palaces rather than museums). What was known during the Napoleonic period as the Empire style, which was characterized by both neoclassical forms and a thematic fixation on Napoleon as a heroic figure, was *authorized* by analogy through actual antiquities from Italy on display in the Musée Napoléon. These objects represented not only ancient Roman glory but also the brute power of Napoleon, whose troops had looted them and undertaken the difficult task of transporting them safely to France. The legitimizing claims for sovereignty in the Musée Napoléon, and the broader neoclassical program of which it was the centerpiece, thus encompassed multiple levels. The raw power to seize artworks and carry them to France (as celebrated by triumphal entry of the Italian works into Paris in 1798 [see fig. 2], for instance) demonstrated Napoleon's famous military prowess, while allegorical curation allowed Napoleon to appropriate the glory not only of the ancient Romans but also of the *ancien régime*, by inserting himself, an upstart, into the same allegorical rhetoric that the Bourbon kings had long used to glorify their reigns. In a statement that says it all, Napoleon's brother Lucien Bonaparte confided to Jacques-Louis David, "My brother is interested only in paintings in which he appears."[29] In short, it was the alienability of cultural property that made it possible for an ambitious soldier like Napoleon to both appropriate the hereditary marks of imperial or absolutist authority *and* simultaneously promulgate a successful cult of personality through the control and manipulation of visual culture. On some level Napoleon's gambit was simple: to transfer the cultural property of France and the world to himself, as his possession.

It is now possible to offer a fuller account of *Art's Properties'* central argument by parsing the double entendre of its title. On the one hand, property may be defined as an entity (either material or immaterial) of which an "owner" claims rights of use, including but not limited to physical possession, and is, conversely, responsible for any claims *against* that property (i.e., liabilities). This question of liability, while generally less prominent in our everyday understanding of ownership, is crucial for appreciating how possession and particularly *self*-possession may be experienced as a burden—an issue that will arise in my discussion of proprietary forms of identity. Because, in practice, the limits of property rights are notoriously slippery, it is more accurate to define proprietorship not as a stable state but as a set of relations. If I own a house with a mortgage, for example, my status as owner is founded on a kind of fiction, authorized by my lender, that the house is "mine"—a fiction that will quickly collapse if I default on the mortgage. However, if a guest slips on my snowy doorstep and injures himself, my responsibility as owner—in the form of a liability—is clear, even if I maintain a large mortgage. As became apparent after the 2008 financial crisis, many mortgages in the United States were bundled and sold as financial instruments, making it even harder to know who might, in fact, own "my" house. If the association of *property* with an entity as seemingly straightforward as a house is unstable, things become more complicated when we consider the second important connotation of *property* in the plural—*properties*, as qualities or attributes. My home, for example, may have two bedrooms, a stucco facade, and a skylight in the living room; it might be sunny, over one hundred years old, and close to public transportation. When we use the term *property*, then, we really mean two things. There is the entity (a "property" in the sense of a house) and its qualities (its characteristics as a sunny, conveniently located, two-bedroom residence in a stucco structure). The category of property is thus divided by an internal fault line: *being* a singular possession and *having* plural qualities or properties. This second dimension of property is a form of *self-possession*: I would not, for example, typically declare that I "own" two bedrooms and a skylight, but rather that I own a house—it is the house that "possesses" those qualities, the bedroom and skylight. The qualities that I properly possess might include whiteness, Jewishness, and queerness. In the matter of real estate, such distinctions may seem merely semantic, but when, in the next section, we consider questions of intellectual property, the question of self-possession, its privileges and liabilities, will be critically important. How then does art function between these two distinct relations of property? I have argued that the fundamental quality of artworks is their constitutive alterity, arising from (1) the structural division between a transitive image and a material substrate; (2) the capacity to give presence to something or someone physically absent; and (3) their unlimited experiential duration through time. In other words, though they are alienable in the sense that they can be bought, sold, or stolen as property, the *properties* of art cannot be exhausted and thus fully consumed, and are, in this sense, inalienable. In my view, art's structural alterity, by which I mean its constitutive instability as a form of representation, disqualifies it from operating effectively in the context of conventional politics. For this reason, I believe that the relation between politics and art inheres neither in the form nor the iconography of an artwork. The politics of art only really begin when an artwork's alterity is captured as a property with properties. The artwork's properties (in the sense of qualities) only become property (in the sense of something owned) when claimed through acts of representation—when, for instance, an artist is said to be French, or "expressionist," or a lesbian. And, as we have seen in our discussion of the Musée Napoléon and the Musée des Monuments Français, representation does not occur once and for all; qualities or attributes may be reorganized in a different configuration of properties when transferred to a new context, as in the two museums. Once physically alienated—when extracted from what Quatremère called their "purpose [*destination*]"—looted artworks were integrated into a new property regime, which their properties were made to represent. In museum galleries, aesthetic properties were harnessed to power through attribution, whether an ancient Roman sculpture was made to allegorically represent Napoleon's glory or an altarpiece to function as a historical document of Renaissance France. It is through the dual forms of art's objectification—as commodity and as representation (through capture and curation, representation, and exchange)—that art enters politics.

Modern Art Was Always Conceptual

In 1793, the same year that the new Louvre opened to the public, the Literary and Artistic Property Act was passed by the National Convention, the parliament of revolutionary France. Also known as the Act of the Rights of Genius, this law was a complement to the Declaration of the Rights of Man and the Citizen (1789), in that it granted artists property rights in the circulation of their creative works. The first article of the 1793 act proclaimed:

> Authors of all kinds of writing, composers of music, painters and draughtsmen who have their paintings reproduced in print shall enjoy a lifetime and exclusive right to sell, authorize for sale and distribute their works in the territory of the Republic, and to transfer that property in full and in part.[1]

The 1793 act was part of a long history of copyright's application to literature and art that began with the Statute of Anne in 1710 and the Engraving Copyright Act of

1735 in Great Britain and continued through the nineteenth century.[2] This gradual shift in the property rights of artists was a logical correlate to the modern museum. For if art no longer belonged to its "purpose [*destination*]," as Quatremère decried, it should belong to its author, who, as an individual proprietor, could and would more easily alienate their "products." Indeed, from the nineteenth century onward, the privileged destination for art would be the museum itself, and in a parallel development, art's commercial structure shifted from personal or governmental patronage, exemplified by the Academic system in France and Great Britain, to an art market. Harrison and Cynthia White call this new environment the "dealer-critic system," and they link its emergence to the Impressionists in the second half of the nineteenth century. According to the Whites, "the focus of the Academic system was not men, not a set of careers, but rather a river of canvases."[3] On the other hand, "It was artists, not paintings, who were the focus of the dealer-critic institutional system.... It dealt with an artist more in terms of his production over a career and thus provided a rational alternative to the chaos of the academic focus on paintings by themselves."[4] The art market, as the site of modern art's ultimate commercial alienability, required an independent proprietor in order to function smoothly. Inherent in the "dealer-critic system" are the two registers of property I articulated earlier: first, the artist has a right to sell their work as a form of property (and protect it against unauthorized reproduction). In this sense the artist is in control of the artwork's transformation into a commodity. This is the "dealer" side of the dealer-critic system. But more important, the *properties* of the artist herself or himself take on a new commercial importance. It is the profile of an artist's *career* that furnishes her or him with marketable properties, and it was precisely the critic's role (as it still is today) to articulate the significance of such properties and to afford the publicity essential to commercial viability. This is how a painting *by* Monet, for instance, becomes "a Monet." The dealer-critic system thus combines the commodification of art as alienable *property* with the *properties* of the artist (their style or career or reputation), which are inalienable. The ownership of a painting by Monet may be transferred from artist to dealer to collector to museum, but through all these transactions it remains "a Monet." We might say that the author "Monet" is the possession of the biographical person, Claude Monet, and in this sense the fundamental property of the artist—the source of his value—is his *self-possession*.

The complex twists and turns of the long development of copyright as applied to literature and art are less important in our context than the broader contours of what was at stake: namely, a shift in the understanding of property according to the ancient model of land tenure (i.e., property as something material—like an estate or artwork) to the immaterial properties of the artist (their concept or invention, or what in the early modern period was called *disegno*). This shift was confirmed, as the Whites recount, in a parallel transformation of the art market from a patronage system that focused on indi-vidual paintings authorized by the Academy to a dealer-critic system that emphasized an artist's creative per-sonality. Because this model of authorship is based on *authorization*—on the guarantee of a work's value by the artist's qualities or properties (their *self-possession*)—it is no surprise that a new model of property distinct from landed estates was invoked by the advocates for expanded copyright protection leading up to the Act of the Rights of Genius. In her account of these debates, Katie Scott describes how a group of printmakers and publishers introduced the *assignat*, or paper money, as an analogy for copyright in their petition to the National Assembly in 1790. The petitioners "were therefore able to argue that, in the same way that one could give, trade, sell or destroy an *assignat* but not forge one, because to do so made a private claim on the portion of the national wealth represented, so one could give, trade, sell or de-stroy prints but could not pirate them."[5] In other words, the source of value in an *assignat* was not its material form but what it represented, and what it represented—somewhat tautologically—authorized its value. In his landmark study on the development of literary copy-right in Britain, Mark Rose makes a similar point: "just as literary property was underwritten by the personality of the author, so the acceptability of commercial paper depended on the credibility of the note issuers and of the endorsers through whose hands they had passed."[6] In short, the transformation of the artist into a propri-etary author—a self-possessed speculator on her or his qualities, or *properties*—put the artist in the position of authorizing their own work as a state authorizes its currency. If rights were granted, their value was nonetheless founded in the credibility—the reputation—of the artist's persona. It is such authorization that is meant by the honorific *genius*.

In 1793, then, the new concepts of the modern museum and the self-possessed artist began to preside over art's value, its capture of alterity. In the museum, this occurred in two ways: first, as recently alienated objects, seized from their proper "purpose [*destination*]," artworks were forced to behave like commodities (whether their exchange was accomplished through plunder or sale). And second, as the constituent elements of a new museology, divorced from their initial function or context, artworks were organized into curatorial narratives based on their various properties, rendering them archival documents or allegories—representations of an era, a nation, or an emperor. The first proprietary model —of universal alienability or exchange—is quantitative and focuses on art as movable property; the second is qualitative (derived from the *properties* of the work) and results in the exchange of meaning through representation. It may seem misguided to categorize *representation* as a mode of creating property, but if, as I have argued, art's ontological fundament is its alterity, then whenever an artwork's dynamic experiential plenitude is made to represent, it ceases to be art and becomes something else—an exchangeable quantum of information. Under modern conditions, art's alterity has become a generator of commodifiable information derived from acts of representation (recall the crush of cell-phone photography in galleries that I invoked in the prologue). And information, of course, has become the premier form of property since the mid-twentieth century. The seed of our information economy, I am arguing, was already present in the Louvre's curatorial reorganization of alienated patrimony. Is it too much to suggest that the museum was an information processor long before the invention of the computer? As we have seen, simultaneous with the emergence of the museum as an apparatus for turning art into information by making it stand for something else—as a document or allegory— was the rise of the self-possessed author whose rights were consolidated through the nineteenth-century development of copyright law and whose reputation as a solitary genius, a Bohemian, or an avant-gardist was an integral product of the dealer-critic system. This kind of author was well suited to the museum, since the proprietary author, like the museum, arises from a convergence of property and representation. In the dealer-critic system, a biographical author like Berthe Morisot could generate a type of property, "a Morisot," over whose creative output the biographical Morisot could claim exclusive rights, while the museum could subsequently introduce her work, within its own proprietary logic, as a representation of a "foremost woman Impressionist."[7] Is it any surprise that paper money—as the perfect elision of commodity and representation—emerged as a metaphor for copyright? The currency of art, like monetary currency, is created through *authorization*, which entails not merely furnishing a work with an author (author-izing it as art) or assigning a work to an author (author-izing them as the artist) but *guaranteeing* the value of art by establishing that an artist is the rightful proprietor of their properties.

I am positing a definition of modern art that derives from two fundamental transformations in art's properties: (1) through its dislocation, looting, or sale, and later in the dealer-critic system, the art object becomes primarily a commodity; and (2) the properties of the artwork are assigned to an author as their property while conversely the author guarantees its value—an author who in turn may represent the properties of a nation, a gender, an ethnicity, and so on. These two transformations in aesthetic property correspond to two new infrastructures: the modern museum and the dealer-critic system. The discursive regime of art c. 1793 was thus already structured according to the two fundamental tenets of Conceptual art as it emerged in the late 1960s and '70s: an acknowledgment of the commodity status of the artwork, and the (ultimately failed) attempt to evade this condition by declaring that the artist's concept—his intellectual property—is the foundation of art, making its material execution superfluous. Conceptual art is often seen as the endpoint of the modern avant-garde and the starting point of what supposedly comes after—which was called postmodernism in the 1980s and '90s and has more recently been periodized as "contemporary art."[8] I would argue that, on the contrary, Conceptual art is consonant with the system of the proprietary artist established c. 1793—in other words, *modern art was always conceptual.* Lawrence Weiner's "Declaration of Intent" (1968), which accompanied many of his works as instruction, may serve as one of the clearest articulations of Conceptual art's embrace of the proprietary artist:

1. The artist may construct the piece.
2. The piece may be fabricated.
3. The piece need not be built.

Each being equal and consistent with the intent of the artist the decision as to condition rests with the receiver upon the occasion of receivership.

Weiner, and many of his cohort, challenged art's commodification, only to root the artwork more firmly in the *artist's properties rather than the property of art as commodity.*[9] Not only was the material substrate of an artwork no longer the locus of its status as property, but materiality was declared irrelevant; it was his "concept" or statement reduced to the barest discursive situation that mattered—that is, mere information. Often Weiner's texts, like the "Declaration of Intent," articulated a state rather than exhorting an action. Something like "A 36 × 36" REMOVAL TO THE LATHING OR SUPPORT WALL OF PLASTER OR WALLBOARD FROM A WALL" (1969) is literally a state-ment—it is the condition of a state as well as a meaningful semantic unit.

There is no tense in this linguistic fragment; we have no way of knowing whether the action it denotes—the removal—has already happened or if it ever will happen in the future. Its happening is in a state of permanent potentiality. But even the attenuated materiality of this statement (not to mention its possible enactments) is ultimately superfluous, since its value pivots on the intention of the artist (which is set free from any particular outcome but nonetheless authorizes that very permission). As Weiner puts it in the "Declaration": "Each being equal and consistent with the intent of the artist." Weiner's elaboration of Conceptual art's self-possession allows others (its receivers) to *execute* the work but not to displace the artist as a source of authorization. Since the value of the work lies in the intention of the artist, and since only Weiner may know his intention, only he may legitimately exercise it. Although posing as permissive, Weiner's system renders any other actor's decision with regard to his works trivial, since *any* of them is consistent with his intention. What one receives in this work is the pure gift of Weiner's intention; in other words, one receives "a Lawrence Weiner," guaranteed by the artist's perfect *self-possession*—his legitimate capacity to *authorize* that property and those properties attached to his name. The receiver might physically execute the work, but she may not *authorize* it—hence, her apparent participation is simultaneously a form of delegation and dispossession. She may execute but not author. The clarity of Weiner's statements offers us a precise definition of the modern artist as that person who can authorize themself as property, and whose self-possession is a valuable form of property. Importantly, though Weiner's staging of the centrality of the self-possessed artist certainly has the quality of an end game, it should not be seen as a revolt against modern art's preceding history (as much of the historiography and criticism of Conceptual art does) but rather as the definitive *realization* of art's modern status as property that, as I have demonstrated, began in earnest c. 1793. For that reason, I think it's fair to claim that modern art has always been conceptual.

If Weiner's project was a logical, even a tautological, conclusion to the convergence of two conditions over two centuries—art's burden of representation pressed into service to offer information about a nation, a gender, or an ethnicity; and the modern artist's becoming-self-possessed as the ultimate guarantee of art's value—then we must interrogate this proprietary form of authorship from a more critical perspective than the conventional celebration of Conceptual art as a politically progressive challenge to art's commodification. On the one hand, the *material attenuations* Weiner accomplished merely shift the locus of commodification from artworks to artists whose self-possession *authorizes* objects as art just as the Treasury Department authorizes US dollars. Indeed, highlighting this shift in art's dominant proprietary relationship seems a more significant contribution on the part of Conceptual art than any disingenuous assault on commodification. After all, Weiner's work and that of his cohort took place at the beginning of a period—the so-called Information Age—whose prosperity was derived from intellectual property, and so the idea of an immaterial product can hardly serve as a critique of commodification but rather its voracious occupation of more and more different forms. But on the other hand, and more importantly, what seems to escape Weiner and his white male colleagues is that self-possession is not a universal capacity. Indeed, Euro-American modernity was built on the systematic dispossession of Indigenous people, enslaved Africans, and the colonized, not to mention the disenfranchisement of women of all ethnicities. It is such *dispossession* that girds the self-possession of patriarchal whiteness.

The history of the period I am sketching—the period of European and North American political and aesthetic modernity—is one in which self-possession came to be seen as the foundation of freedom. As C. B. Macpherson demonstrated in his influential account of "possessive individualism," from Hobbes through Locke personhood was defined by property in oneself. This primary self-possession is what allows a person to alienate their labor to accumulate external forms of property, like crops and estates. Michel Foucault updated this conception of "possessive individualism" with his declaration that *"Homo oeconomicus* is an entrepreneur, the entrepreneur of himself,"[10] a neoliberal subject that not merely possesses themself but speculates on their educational and cultural properties as social capital to accumulate wealth more effectively.

In discussing the vicious circle of "possessive individualism," Macpherson concisely summarizes its double bind: "The initial equality of natural rights, which consisted in no man having jurisdiction over another cannot last after the differentiation of property. To put it in another way, the man without property in things loses that full proprietorship of his own person which was the basis of his equal natural rights."[11] Conversely, those without proprietorship in their person could not bear rights. What Macpherson somewhat coyly calls the "differentiation of property" might be rephrased as the accumulation of capital through the dispossession of others—laborers, people of color, women, and so on. A responsible history of modernity and modern art must explore how the authorial self-possession upon which the museum-dealer-critic complex depended, was premised on the dispossession of those defined as not fully self-possessed but rather the partial or full property of others. As we have already seen, the Musée Napoléon was built on the dispossession of both the French *ancien régime* and Napoleon's European enemies. But art's participation in dispossession reaches far beyond these "near" others, these other Europeans.

Robert Nichols has proposed a precise definition of dispossession in his book *Theft Is Property!* He writes, "'dispossession' may be coherently reconstructed to refer to a process in which new proprietary relations are generated but under structural conditions that demand their simultaneous negation. In effect, the dispossessed come to 'have' something they cannot use, except by alienating it to another."[12] Nichols applies this definition to the differing experiences of dispossession among Native peoples and African Americans in the United States. Among the former, who are his primary concern, the double bind of dispossession plays out over the rights to ancestral lands. Traditionally, Native territory was not held as private property but conceived of as a living entity, even a kind of person, and thus was inalienable and impossible to commodify. However, when making claims to the US government for control over their territory, Native activists are forced into the absurd position of claiming ownership of land they believe *cannot be owned*. Nichols explains this contradiction in terms of the paradox of dispossession by which "the dispossessed come to 'have' something they cannot use, except by alienating it to another." Because the matrix of private property is epistemologically incommensurable with how land is held in common in Indigenous traditions, dispossession is accomplished *by imposing a regime of property upon them*, thus ascribing formal rights to them that in practice exist only to be violated, thus affording a patina of legitimacy to acts of appropriation. As Nichols puts it:

> It is not *only* that the earth has been commodified, privatized, and 'enclosed' but that colonization generates a form of commodification so as to divest Indigenous peoples *in a distinct and particular way* of their

ancestral homes. The duality of this process (propertization and systemic theft) is what the concept of dispossession is meant to capture.[13]

Nichols demonstrates something crucially important: that under modern Western conditions, the property relation is *compulsory*—a proprietary person is the only kind of subject legible under the law in liberal democracies. Consequently, indigenous epistemologies are rendered incoherent and can be "legitimately" abrogated by Western courts. Dispossession is not, therefore, the condition of lacking property altogether but, rather, the perversion of self-possession from an asset into a liability. All subjects of modern states, no matter how attenuated their personhood is under the law, can only become intelligible *as persons* through the prism of property. Consequently, dispossession is not the state of lacking a proprietary self but rather a form of self-possession that functions as a liability.

If the locus of dispossession for Native Americans is the land, Nichols follows Saidiya Hartman and other influential Black feminists such as Patricia Williams and Hortense Spillers in arguing that the dispossession of enslaved people was sited in their persons. Hartman has brilliantly articulated how slavery perverted possessive individualism through the enslaved's status as both possession and person. In her account, she takes great pains to avoid characterizing this condition as one of absolute dispossession—or social death. Instead, the contradiction of the dual status of the enslaved is diagnosed not as the *absence* of personhood but rather as a particularly cruel reorganization of the relation between person and property across a spectrum that Alexander Weheliye has enumerated as "full humans, not-quite-humans, and nonhumans."[14] Whereas, for a normative white subject (in the nineteenth century and still to this day), self-possession is typically experienced as an asset—for the enslaved it was a liability. This is because enslaved Africans were granted the status of persons under the law only when they broke it. This could occur, as Hartman recounts, by literally "stealing themselves away,"[15] escaping the plantation either for an evening out to attend a party or in search of permanent freedom in the North. Similarly, when an enslaved individual committed a crime, the state assigned him or her the legal liability ascribed to persons under law, despite their lack of formal rights in every other regard. Hence, it was only as a criminal or a fugitive that the enslaved attained personhood. As Hartman writes:

> Not surprisingly, the agency of the enslaved is only intelligible or recognizable as crime and the designation of personhood burdened with incredible duties and responsibilities that serve to enhance the repressive mechanisms of power, denote the limits of socially tolerable forms of violence, and intensify and legitimate violence in the guise of protection, justice, and the recognition of slave humanity. This official acknowledgment of agency and humanity, rather than challenging or contradicting the object status and absolute

subjugation of the enslaved as chattel, reinscribes it in the terms of personhood.[16]

Hartman does not *oppose* person to property but rather demonstrates how personhood is unevenly distributed to create self-possession as a liability rather than an asset among the enslaved. Her formulation is therefore consistent with Nichols's definition of dispossession as a social dynamic by which the dispossessed "come to 'have' something they cannot use, except by alienating it to another." For when the law is transgressed, the bondage of slavery is exchanged, through the "humanization" of the enslaved, for the bondage of criminality.

Crucially—and tragically—the nineteenth-century racialization of self-possession, which occurred not only in the United States, through slavery and the colonization of Indigenous peoples, but also in Europe's imperial adventures around the world, made the possession of whiteness into an economic asset, while Blackness and Indigeneity functioned as economic liabilities. Scholars like Cheryl Harris, George Lipsitz, Stephen Best, and Aileen Moreton-Robinson, among others, have demonstrated that the property of whiteness continues to disproportionately produce material prosperity and legal recognition at the expense of people of color. Harris's work has been particularly influential in establishing a chain of proprietary associations between whiteness, property, personhood, and freedom. Moreover, she, like Mamdani and Nichols, constructs a field of racialized personhood that encompasses both African American and Indigenous people. In her groundbreaking 1993 essay "Whiteness as Property," she writes:

> Slavery as a system of property facilitated the merger of white identity and property. Because the system of slavery was contingent on and conflated with racial identity, it became crucial to be "white," to be identified as white, to have the property of being white. Whiteness was the characteristic, the attribute, the property of free human beings.... Similarly, the settlement and seizure of Native American land supported white privilege through a system of rights in land in which the "race" of the Native Americans rendered their first possession rights invisible and justified conquest.[17]

In the course of my argument thus far, I have distinguished two registers of property: the commodification of material entities—like artworks—that are subject to exchange; and a proprietary form of representation, by which, for instance, artworks are transformed into information by staging them as documents or allegories—of a period, a person, or place—within a curatorial narrative. It is worth noting the presence of these dual registers in Harris's analysis as well. On the one hand, she argues that whiteness is an asset that leads to the disproportionate accumulation of wealth by those who possess it—in other words, it is a kind of commodity that can be speculated on. This is the argument of George Lipsitz in his book *The Possessive Investment in Whiteness*.

Lipsitz describes the systematic economic dispossession of African American communities in the twentieth century through, for instance, discriminatory federal housing policies favoring white people, environmental racism, and systematic disinvestment in urban neighborhoods, including schools, where large numbers of Black people live. In this regard, whiteness functions as a real asset, and Blackness as a real liability. But Harris is also attentive to the value of whiteness as a proprietary form of *representation*. She argues that whiteness comes to *represent* personhood, through both slavery's association of the nonperson with Blackness and the racialized projection of inferiority onto Native Americans as a justification to nullify their traditional rights to territory. But there is a third consequence of "Whiteness as Property." In discussing affirmative action cases, Harris argues that their adjudication often hinges on the alleged harm to an individual white plaintiff, who claims that the denial of admission to a university, for instance, is the result of an unfair consideration given a student of color. As a result of this *personalization*, in which the question becomes one of compensation for harms done to an individual, the *systemic* structure of racism, defined as the uneven outcomes it generates for entire classes of people—such as African Americans—goes unrecognized. Harris describes this dynamic as follows:

> I examine how the property interest in whiteness has skewed the concept of affirmative action by focusing on the sin or innocence of individual white claimants with

vested rights as competitors of Blacks whose rights are provisional and contingent, rather than on the broader questions of distribution of benefits and burdens. This focus improperly narrows the affirmative action debate to corrective/compensatory issues, to the exclusion of distributive issues. Asking distributive questions about affirmative action is not only conceptually warranted but it is an effective beginning to disentangling whiteness from property through refocusing on the extent to which the existing distorted distribution results directly from racial subordination.[18]

Harris's account of how affirmative action cases reduce systemic discrimination to individual instances of harm, introduces a distinct form of representation, which I have yet to consider in discussing how personal properties may represent assets or liabilities. As the living sign of a broader community, the individual claimant stands in for a constituency to which she or he has no formal legal ties or responsibility: a white person represents all white people, or a Black person denotes Blackness. In the legal systems of liberal democracy, it is overwhelmingly individuals to whom claims may be addressed and upon whom claims of responsibility may be made, and therefore to address a systemic problem, the law typically ends up addressing individual persons. In other words, the individual represents the collective by exhibiting its properties (e.g., skin color, nationality, political affiliation). Mahmood Mamdani, among others, has broadened this critique of the *personalization* of responsibility to the wider scale of human rights. He argues that the way war crimes, genocide, and civil wars are worked through in institutions such as truth and reconciliation commissions tends, like affirmative action, to individualize the responsibility for systemic forms of violence or harm. In his view, for instance, it was a mistake to situate criminal culpability in individual Nazis *as representatives of Nazism tout court* in the Nuremberg trials. He concludes: "At Nuremberg, and now in the mission statements and rules governing institutions from Human Rights Watch to the International Criminal Court, the injustice wrought by states was depoliticized and repackaged as the responsibility of specific people who had done wrong or authorized others to do wrong."[19] What he means here by depoliticization, is that the politics and policies of Nazism, which included not only many complicit constituencies within Germany but others far beyond its borders, could be left uninterrogated, and largely untouched, if a few exemplary individuals were addressed as the responsible agents.[20] More than this, the individual Nazis prosecuted for war crimes represented the responsibility or liability of the group with which they were identified. Like Harris, Mamdani highlights a central feature of liberalism, which has intensified under neoliberal conditions: the uncompromising assignment of responsibility to individuals for the harms they may perpetrate or experience. Systemic forms of dispossession—ranging from National Socialism to contemporary forms of white supremacy—are consequently represented as the crimes of individual persons. Likewise, the neoliberal dismantling of the welfare state since the late 1970s (roughly contemporaneous with Conceptual art's influence) has been justified ideologically by the insistence that the poor bear the responsibility for their failure to thrive. As Mamdani argues, the personalization of systemic problems removes them from the realm of politics and into the context of criminality, and thus forecloses the possibility of political solutions; or, as Harris puts it, issues of distributive justice give way to isolated correctives or compensation. In other words, the property of personhood stands in for the social; the individual *represents* politics while acting as the agent of its neutralization. This larger shift in the individual person as the privileged addressable political unit (as opposed to, for instance, classes, tribes, or even political parties) leads to what Sylvia Wynter calls the overrepresentation of "Man." For Wynter, it is the narration of personhood, or different *genres* of the human, that establishes relations of power. Consequently, for her, as for Michel Foucault,[21] "Man" is not a universal transhistorical category but one that arose in the modern era, originating in the secular humanism of the Renaissance. This modern genre of the human shifted medieval Christianity's primary experience of alterity between God and Man to a terrestrial one, in which a profoundly racialized form of otherness authorized Europe's colonial conquests. Alterity thus shifted from a vertical axis between Man on earth to God in the heavens to a horizontal one, based on different, hierarchically ranked genres of the human. Wynter writes:

> In the wake of the West's reinvention of its True Christian Self in the transumed terms of the Rational Self of Man, however, it was to be the peoples of the militarily expropriated New World territories (i.e., Indians), as well as the enslaved peoples of Black Africa (i.e., Negroes), that were made to reoccupy the matrix slot of Otherness—to be made into the physical referent of the idea of the irrational/subrational Human Other, to this first degodded (if still hybridly religio-secular) "descriptive statement" of the human in history, as the descriptive statement that would be foundational to modernity.[22]

The power of this "Man" is exercised through its overrepresentation, she asserts: "Man overrepresents itself as if it were the human itself: overrepresentation is the strategy of survival of the Western Bourgeois."[23] In other words, overrepresentation is that tendency to personify the collective that I noted in Harris's and Mamdani's critiques of affirmative action and human rights discourse. As Wynter argues, the overrepresentation of the white subject thus extinguishes other genres of the human by rendering them illegible. In our context, it is worth questioning whether the modern *artist*, as a kind of person whose self-possession is particularly complete, and whose creative liberty exemplifies the neoliberal entrepreneur of oneself, might be an agent of over-representation. Or, put more polemically, is the modern (and contemporary) artist the privileged representative of "Man" (as Wynter describes that figure, as a disfiguration of the human grounded in patriarchal whiteness)?

Indeed, Lawrence Weiner's claim to absolute possession of his aesthetic intention and the power he exercises to authorize it seem to epitomize Wynter's genre of "Man" as the perfectly self-possessed individual. I want to be clear that I am not suggesting that Weiner was personally racist, or in any way intentionally harmful in his individual behavior, or that he was acting in bad faith as an artist. I have no evidence of any such wrongdoing, nor do I mean to insinuate it. For as Harris and Mamdani demonstrate, the greatest harms occur on a systemic level, rather than through the acts of individuals, whose intentions vary and, *pace* Weiner, are largely unknowable. While the art world as well as the discipline of art history tend to overrepresent the agency of individual artists, systemic harm, like white supremacy, should be measured by the uneven outcomes that result from it, and one can hardly claim that the art world c. 1970 did not exclude most artists who didn't look like Weiner. This, however, does not mean that alternate and resistant voices were not present. In a nearly contemporaneous series of works under the title *Catalysis* (1970–73), the African American artist Adrian Piper developed a practice of what we might call systematic self-*dispossession* (fig. 3). This series involved Piper making her body repugnant in some way and then moving about in public. In various works in the series, for instance, she soiled her clothes with foul smells and then rode the subway and browsed a bookstore; she inserted a towel in her mouth and traveled on a city bus; and while doing research at a library she carried a concealed tape recording of periodic loud belches. These works were minimally documented, and the locus of their aesthetic experience was in the encounter with others. As Piper wrote in 1971:

> I define the work as the viewer's reaction to it. The strongest, most complex, and most aesthetically interesting catalysis is the one that occurs in uncategorized, undefined, nonpragmatic human confrontation. The immediacy of the artist's presence as an artwork/catalysis confronts the viewer with a broader, more powerful, and more ambiguous situation than discrete forms and objects.[24]

Practically every dimension of Weiner's Conceptual proposition is here reversed. In place of an authoritative statement of intention, Piper initiates an open-ended catalysis, resulting in confrontations that are beyond the artist's control. If Weiner functions as an absent author of statements that embody his intentions, Piper's body must be present for the work to exist. Her physicality is the catalyst, while Weiner's is irrelevant vis-à-vis his work. And yet, far from guaranteeing self-possession,

Piper's embodiment marks her dispossession—she is not acting as "Adrian Piper," or even as a generic "Black woman," but rather as an anonymous member of an abject genre of the not-quite-human. With the addition of her repulsive props, she is neither herself nor fully a person. But this alienation of her identity—her name as an artist, as it were—is twinned with her delegation of authority over the work to chance encounters, the openness of an unfolding event. As a catalyst, she only initiates and cannot control the outcome of her work. In place of Weiner's "receiver," who enjoys the apparent choice of how to realize a piece—a choice rendered nugatory, since the artist has granted his permission in advance to any rendering whatsoever—Piper is dispossessed as an authoritative artist because, as she puts it, "I define the work as the viewer's reaction to it." As different as Weiner and Piper's works are, they both explore a historically specific crisis in personhood, pivoting on the limits of self-possession strongly inflected by their different positions as white man and African American woman. In Weiner's case, this crisis is manifest in the attenuation of the artist's manual plenitude through the delegation of his work's realization to others (perhaps under the growing pressure of information technologies). The confidence he displays in authorizing his artistic intention as a form of property veils a profound pessimism about one's capacity to control the form of an object—even an art object—once it begins to circulate. His solution, as we have seen, is to devalue the material rendition of works while overvaluing the artist's intention. The crisis in personhood that Piper manifests encompasses Weiner's skepticism about objectification, but for her, authoritative control over her "own" artistic intention seems unattainable or undesirable. Since this abdication of control is paired with an abjection of her person, and in light of her later projects, which explicitly racialize self-possession, what is catalyzed in *Catalysis* is an *exposure* of the precarity of the artist's personhood, strongly inflected by her experience of Blackness, rather than an assertion of its plenitude.

I declared, in the title of this section, that "Modern Art Was Always Conceptual." I believe this to be true because the crisis in personhood that I have traced in Weiner's and Piper's work has characterized Euro-American modern art from its beginnings. As we have seen, in the course of the nineteenth century, the property of art was no longer defined by a specific "purpose," as Quatremère had put it, from which artworks derived their meaning (i.e., a church or palace), nor as the century wore on, were artists primarily patronized by individual benefactors or through the Academic system. The modern artist became self-possessed: she served as her own purpose and her own patron in the marketplace of the dealer-critic system. But what exactly does it mean to be self-possessed? It is an absurdity to suggest that a human being has legal title to themself, and even if this were possible, how does one determine the contours of a self? Does it encompass more than a body, everything produced by the person? Is every word of internal monologue susceptible to capture or protection as property? In my view, the only way to define self-possession coherently is as a by-product of representation. In entering an abortion clinic, a woman represents herself as the individual who can authorize a medical procedure on the body she "possesses." She does this by producing representations, like a driver's license, that the state has issued to authorize the attachment of her name to her body. There really is no ground to property in oneself, except as an accumulation of representations. But the nature of representation is no less slippery than that of self-possession. I have stated above that representation occurs when one thing stands in for another, but we know from semiotics that such signifying links are arbitrary and from politics that they may be deeply deceptive. It is for this reason that the theorist F. R. Ankersmit describes political representation as *aesthetic*. He argues that since there can be no identity between a representative and those she represents (this would constitute direct democracy, as opposed to representative government), the process of representation must always be artificially crafted and, consequently, belongs to the realm of the aesthetic. To press his point, Ankersmit describes democratic procedures in terms of the art-historical category of medium: "In the political representation process, a depiction of a political will that exists in one medium (the people) is made visible and present in another medium (the representative body)."[25] In politics, as in art, representation is not transparently mimetic—rather, it translates between two distinct "media," and as no translation can ever be considered definitive, nor can any representation. Consequently, any representation, no matter how literal, is a kind of invention—this is why Ankersmit calls political forms of representation *aesthetic*.

What is most striking in Ankersmit's account is his assertion that political power arises at precisely the moment that a link is established between a representation and that which is represented. In other words, power does not preexist its representation; politically, it inheres in neither the people nor their delegates but in the aesthetic association of the two:

> The political reality created by aesthetic representation is therefore essentially political *power*. The aesthetic difference or gap between the represented and his or her representative is the origin of (legitimate) political power, and we are therefore justified in assigning to political power an *aesthetic* rather than *ethical* nature.[26]

It is important to recognize here that Ankersmit theorizes power as an effect of the *space of representation*, and he defines that space *as a kind of gap*. As he puts it, "power originates neither in the people … nor the ruler … but *between* the people and the state."[27] Similarly, in the context of Weiner's and Piper's work, the degree of authoritative personhood each artist represents—the position they occupy on Weheliye's spectrum of "full humans, not-quite-humans, and nonhumans"—emerges from a "difference or gap." For Weiner this gap is the virtual space that divides his statements from their potential material execution by others, and consequently generates the power of his artistic intention, whereas in *Catalysis* it is the physical space of encounter between Piper's performing body and the strangers she meets by chance that accrues the power of an abject body—coded as Black—to evacuate the intentionality of the artist and concede it to others, rather than delegating it as Weiner does. These are two different constituent moments of personhood with two quite different effects: self-possession on the one hand and dispossession on the other. If Conceptual art is defined, then, as an assertion or interrogation of possessive individualism through the artist's representation of their properties as those of the world (whether characterized by authoritative intentionality in the case of Weiner or the precarity of social exposure in the case of Piper), then I think it's reasonable to say that modern art has always been conceptual. This is because modern art has consistently staged the assertion of self-possession as means of over-representing "Man" in its precarity—its violence, its narcissism, its class struggles and pretensions, its erotic adventures, its white supremacy, and so on. Modern art has consistently served as a laboratory for the aesthetic dimension of modernity's regime of possessive individualism. Indeed, following Ankersmit, we could describe the power of European painting of the nineteenth century as arising in the gap between the individual properties of the artist—their aesthetic sensibility—and the historical or empirical properties of the world.

In projecting their perceptual framework onto reality, the artist claims the world as their property in an instance of overrepresentation that instantiates Wynter's figure of "Man." From this perspective, a highly schematic genealogy of modern art during the nineteenth century might be sketched as follows: Romanticism, in which an artist's distinctive painterly style, as exemplified, for instance, by Eugène Delacroix's agitated brushstroke, is associated with their personality in a newly intimate way, but this temperament becomes the lens through which to represent events drawn both from contemporary politics and the history of literature, thus fusing a singular way of seeing with historicism to produce visual narratives quite distinct from the Academic orthodoxy of the *ancien régime.* Mid-nineteenth century Realism is in many ways an aesthetic readjustment of Romanticism, favoring objective empiricism over subjective temperament, while continuing to maintain the essential association between them and without minimizing the importance of the artist's personality, as in the case of Gustave Courbet, who did a great deal to promote his own work and Realism as a style. Impressionism transposes the issues of a historically inflected experience of personhood onto a more self-consciously optical register. Regarding the *impression*, for instance, as a particular kind of mark made by the artists historically grouped as Impressionists, the art historian Richard Shiff has demonstrated how the gap between subjectivity and objectivity is bridged materially in each deposit of paint, or "impression." He writes, "The impression . . . is the embryo of both bodies of one's knowledge, subjective knowledge of the self and objective knowledge of the world; it exists prior to the realization of the subject/object distinction."[28] An impression is a painterly mark that simultaneously registers an objective optical effect—an empirically accurate registration of light effects—and a subjective temperament, or the artist's characteristic way of seeing. In other words, the Impressionist represents at once the artist's personal properties (their visual temperament) and the property of the world, by capturing the evanescent qualities of a landscape or cityscape. In the historical avant-gardes of the early and mid-twentieth century, the tie between opticality and subjectivity was intensified by some artists in various forms of abstract painting (ranging from Wassily Kandinsky to Kazimir Malevich) and rejected by others in favor of modes of chance linked superficially or profoundly to dreams and the unconscious, by which Dadaists and Surrealists tied the liberation of one's personal drives and desires—the unconscious—to political liberty and social revolution. Others submerged their personal sensibility into the rationality of the engineer or propagandist in order to model a utopian or revolutionary world (Constructivists, De Stijl). But always present is the subject/object divide that constitutes the overrepresented bourgeois white subject as "Man"—tying temperamental/optical/psychological/ideological self-possession to the capacity to represent the world, thus assuming the mantle of the universal human, the genre of "Man." Conceptual art only further abstracts the dynamic that has characterized modern art from the beginning—its articulation of the struggle for self-possession as one that must impose the artist's properties (an intention) on the material world (as property). Of course, the relationship between the psychological properties of an artist and the material means by which they represent the human have varied greatly over time. But the constituent moment of linking intention to matter and claiming the product not only as art but as the evidence of "Man" as a cultured being with a usable heritage has characterized modern art from the beginning, and in this sense it has always been conceptual.

And yet, as Wynter shows and Piper demonstrates in her *Catalysis* series, the genre of the human that is "Man" abandons a broad class of persons who were excluded from the category of humanity (and its exemplary manifestation as the artist) for most of the history of Euro-American art. Afro-pessimists such as Frank B. Wilderson III have influentially argued that Blackness, in its persistent association with slavery, continues to signify the nonhuman to this day. He writes:

> Thus modernity marks the emergence of a new ontology because it is an era in which an entire race appears, people who, a priori, that is prior to the contingency of the "transgressive act" (such as losing a war or being convicted of a crime), stand as socially dead in relation to the rest of the world.[29]

He goes on to declare that "the Human was born, but not before it murdered the Black, forging a symbiosis between the political ontology of Humanity and the social death of Blacks."[30] As defined by Orlando Patterson, the social death of slavery that Wilderson alludes to was related not to the question of forced labor nor even to the enslaved's status as property. Rather, it was due to what Patterson called *natal alienation*, defined as the dissolution and delegitimation of all relations of kinship among the enslaved and, more broadly, their radical dispossession from an African (or any other) heritage.[31] This is not to say that enslaved individuals did not create communities and loving familial relations as well as a rich culture within the strictures of the plantation, but that these relations and this culture were neither legally recognized nor respected in practice by whites—and indeed, intimate relationships among the enslaved were liberally transgressed, as when a slaveholder would sell children away from their mothers.

In other words, like the alienated artifacts that Napoleon captured, accumulated, and curated as a fundamental means of asserting his imperial power, Africans, both the enslaved in the Americas and colonial subjects in their native lands, were conceived by white people as alienable properties, both economically (through slave labor and colonial exploitation) and symbolically (through the exaltation and definition of white self-possession by way of the "possession" of people of color). This analogy between alienated artworks (which, as I have argued, stood in for or represented subject cultures) and natally alienated human beings is not merely metaphorical. In the European and American world expositions of the late nineteenth and early twentieth centuries, so-called human zoos were frequently inserted amid exhibits of European industry and culture, drawing comparisons between advanced technology and "primitive" peoples that implicitly demonstrate their economic and ideological interdependence (fig. 4). Reconstructed villages or streets were displayed in Paris or Chicago and inhabited by residents of colonial territories who were brought to the Euro-American metropole to enact their daily lives before crowds of white spectators. As one visitor to the 1900 Exposition Universelle in Paris described:

> Here are multi-colored dwellings of the various Asiatic and African natives subject to the dominion of France…. Here one may sit and take tea or coffee, served by men of strange tropical nationalities, whose faces look as polished as your fire-grate at home…. Some of these people have never before worn clothes, and even now wear them much against their will. Amongst the many different villages of huts or Kraals built here by each tribe according to its native custom, that of the French dependency of Senegal is probably the one that attracts the most visitors. In this little village of jet-black negroes are men and youths of different ages, several women, and even children.[32]

Added to the humiliation of their exhibition before gaping European spectators in the role of "creatures" in a human zoo (who are thereby rendered ethically acceptable as "colonial possessions") is a second order of captivity. The "various Asiatic and African natives" at the exposition were not only enclosed by fences but also captured as images—images to which, as Frantz Fanon devastatingly theorized, Black people in general were enslaved. As Fanon wrote in *Black Skin, White Masks*, published in 1952: "I am overdetermined from the outside. I am a slave not to the 'idea' others have of me, but to my appearance."[33] The "strange tropical nationalities" who allegedly clothed themselves only reluctantly, may have been only temporary resident-prisoners of the Paris fairgrounds, but they were more enduringly chained to the racist stereotypes developed by colonial powers to legitimize their power.

In the course of this book I have often dwelled on the desire to capture images, which is shared by contemporary museumgoers wielding cell-phone cameras and the emperor Napoleon alike, but I have focused less, until now, on the converse dynamic: how images may be deployed to capture humans. As Fanon argues, the racist stereotype "overdetermines" those who are targeted, and these persons must contend with the representation by which they are "enslaved." Fanon's reversal of the normative relation between an image and a human—that the former is the possession or product of the latter—introduces a crucial and paradoxical dimension of visual property. For although the enslaving image, as Fanon theorizes it, oppresses its human object, it is nonetheless an inalienable property of that person—once a stereotype has been established, it becomes a fact with which the stereotyped must deal. Power, as Ankersmit teaches us, arises between the representation and the represented. The stereotype produces a "second self" with which its object must deal. Fanon, the theorist, philosopher, and psychiatrist, describes this dilemma as an encounter with a Black stereotype—the bellhop—at the movies:

> I can't go to the movies without encountering myself. I wait for myself. Just before the film starts, I wait for myself. Those in front of me look at me, spy on me, wait for me. A black bellhop is going to appear. My aching heart makes my head spin.[34]

What Fanon describes is the personification of dispossession: the confrontation with a virtual double for which one is responsible. Here is the double bind that people of color have experienced in the European diaspora: their dispossession has functioned as a negative possession, a permanent liability. They have no choice but to "own" the stereotype and to try to find a way beyond it. This is precisely what the pioneering sociologist W.E.B. Du Bois did at the 1900 Paris exposition by organizing a small multimedia exhibition titled *Nègres d'Amerique,* installed in the Pavilion of Social Economy.[35] This exhibition countered the pseudo-ethnographic installations of colonial peoples with two distinctly different visual languages: data visualization, in the form of charts communicating various aspects of African American life, and photographic documentation, including pictures of African American educational institutions and businesses and many portraits of individuals. Among the most powerful graphics was *Proportion of Negroes in the Total Population of the United States*, in which a small, solid black figure of the contours of the United States was placed within a larger red outline of that nation in order to indicate the proportion of African American citizens (fig. 5). Similarly, Du Bois described the collection of photographs he assembled as a "small nation of people picturing their life and development without apology or gloss, and above all made by themselves."[36] In other words, in an act of resistance to being enslaved by their images, these subjects posed as proper, educated, respectable citizens of a "small nation of people," a nation within a nation, while Du Bois's analytical charts replaced the visceral experience of "primitivism" in the human zoo with an analytics of structural dispossession *and* the progress made in redressing it. This small, scholarly display was certainly no match for the spectacle of the human zoo, but their juxtaposition delineates the fundamental dynamic of modern art that I have been elaborating in the course of this book: the two-part operation of capture and curation. Du Bois fought images with images. In the face of a dominant condition of dispossession among Africans and African Americans, he deployed the genres of data visualization and portraiture as opposed to the genre of racist ethnography. This tactic has profound significance to this day, for it suggests that to make visible a new genre of the human, new *aesthetic* genres are required, a new aesthetics of power.

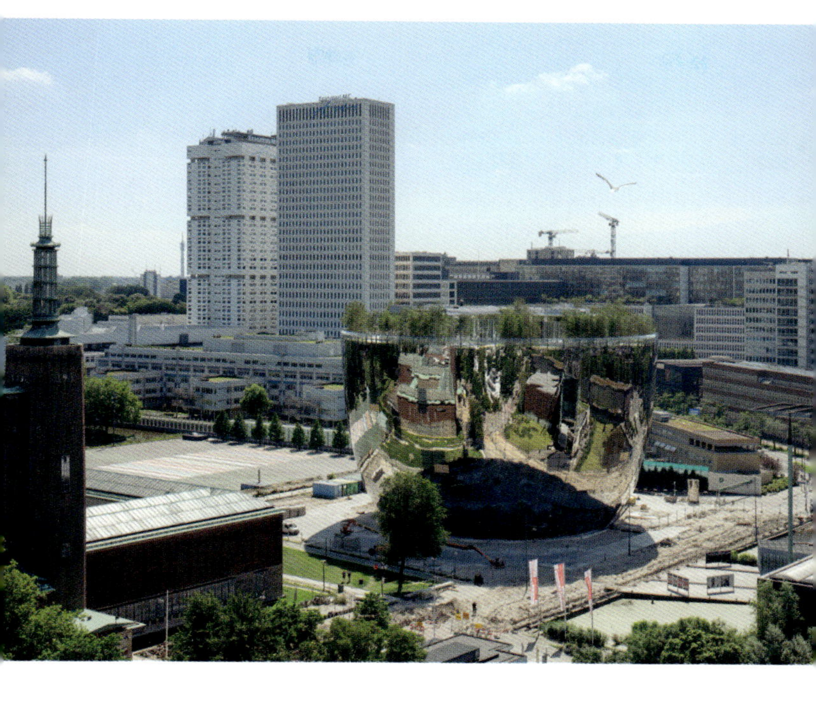

FIGURE 1. MVRDV Architects, Depot Boijmans Van Beuningen, Rotterdam, opened November 2021.

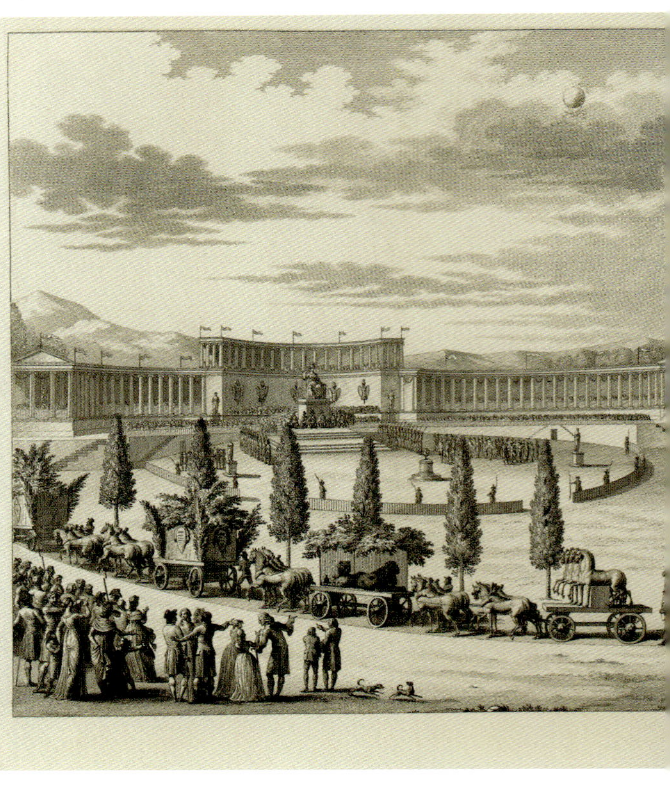

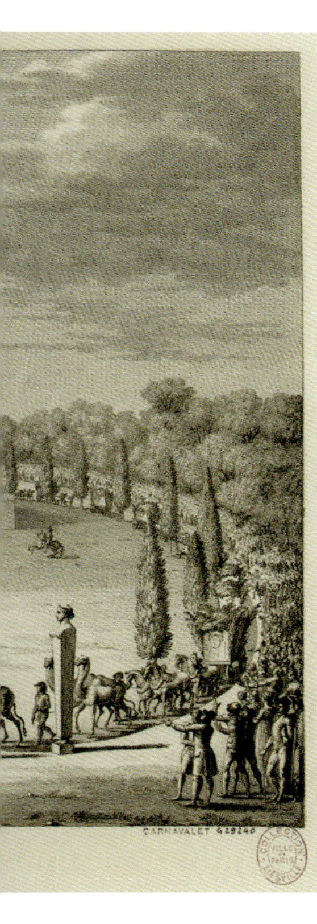

FIGURE 2. Pierre-Gabriel Berthault, *Entrée Triomphale des monuments des sciences et des arts en France*, c. 1793–1803. Print, 13 × 19½ in. (32.8 × 49.4 cm).

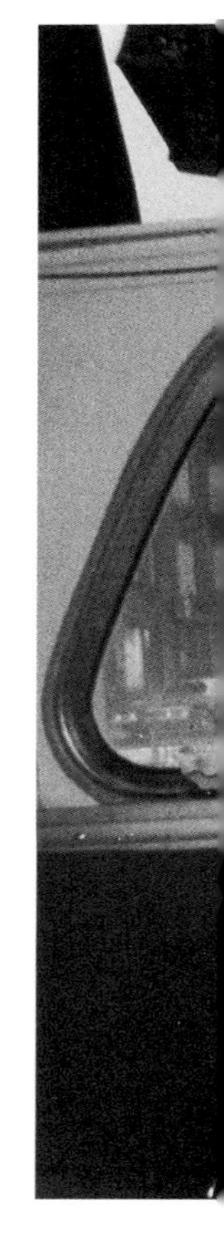

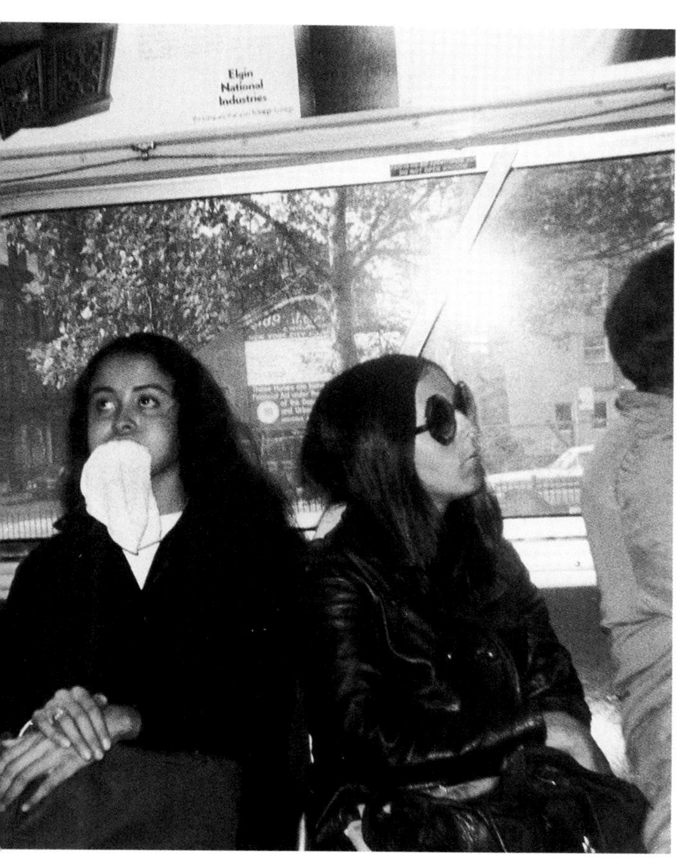

FIGURE 3. Adrian Piper, *Catalysis IV*, 1971. Documentation of the performance, black-and-white photograph, silver gelatin on baryta paper (printed c. 1998), 16 × 16 in. (41 × 41 cm).

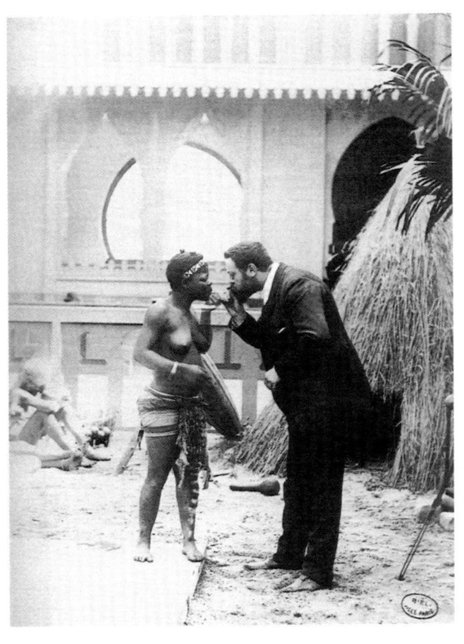

FIGURE 4. *Rencontre Insolite*, Exposition Universelle, Paris, 1900.

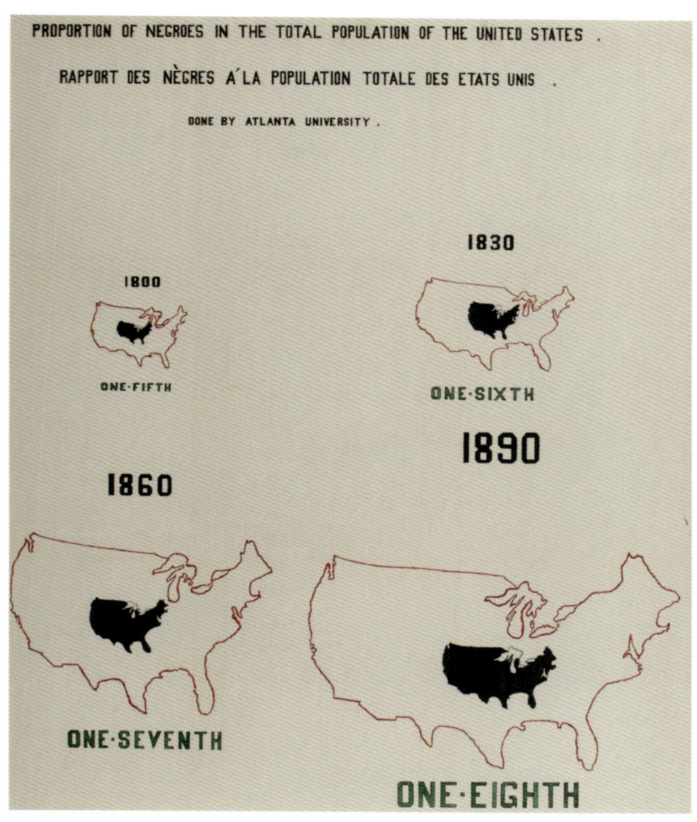

FIGURE 5. W.E.B. Du Bois and Atlanta University, [*A Series of Statistical Charts Illustrating the Condition of the Descendants of Former African Slaves Now in Residence in the United States of America*] *Proportion of Negroes in the Total Population of the United States*, 1900. Ink and watercolor, 28 × 22 in. (71 × 56 cm).

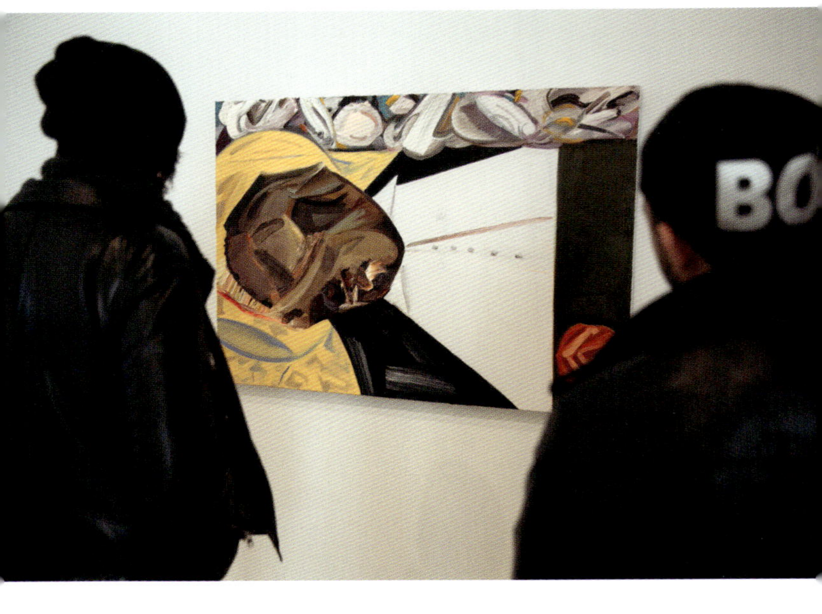

Figure 6. Installation view of Dana Schutz, *Open Casket*, 2016. Oil on canvas, 39 × 53 in. (99 × 130 cm), Whitney Museum of American Art, New York.

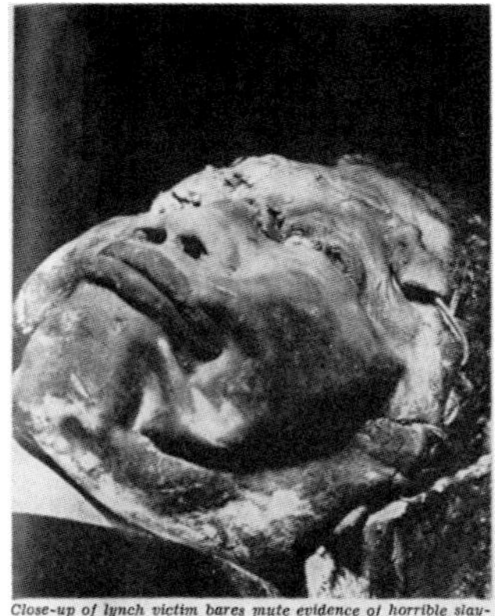

FIGURE 7. Emmett Till in his casket. From *Jet Magazine*, September 15, 1955.

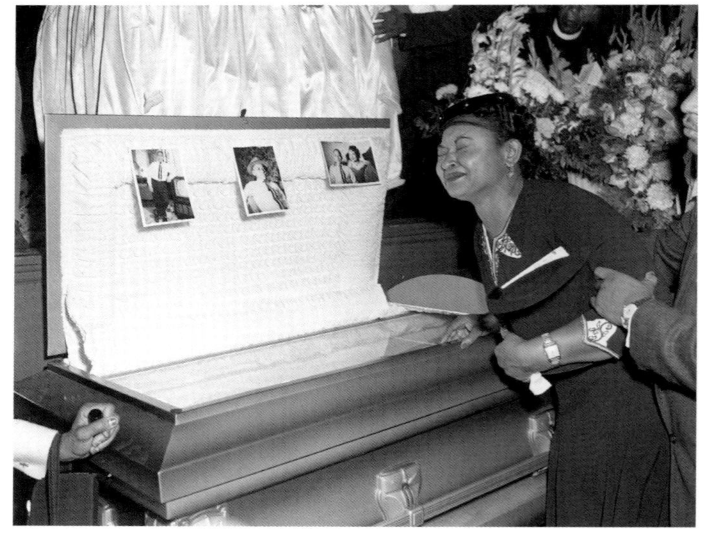

FIGURE 8. Mamie Till-Mobley at Emmett's funeral wearing his watch, September 3, 1955. Taped to the casket are photographs from their last Christmas together.

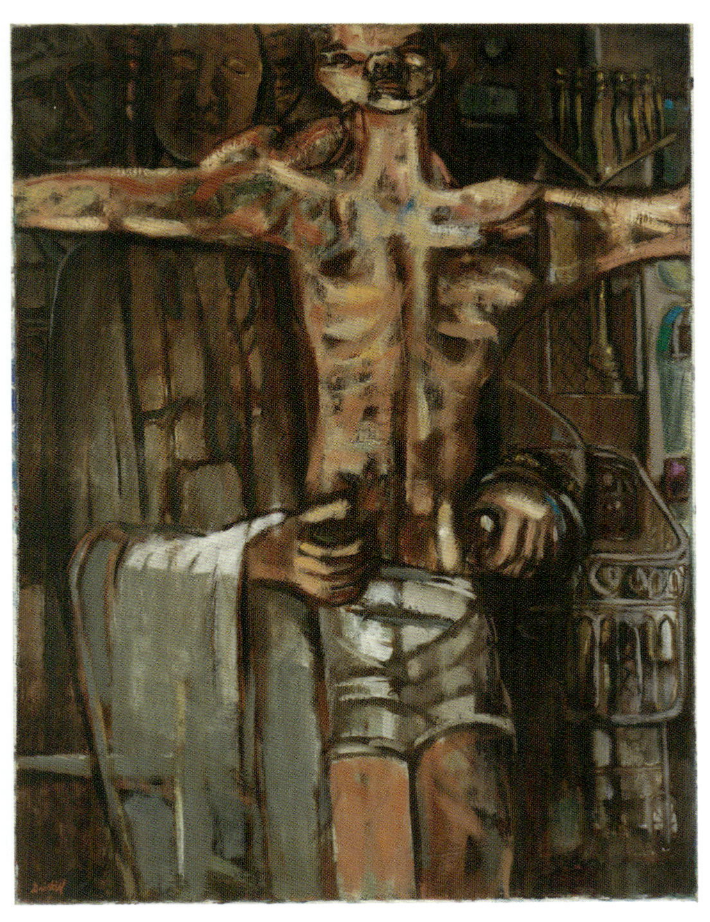

FIGURE 9. David Driskell, *Behold Thy Son*, 1956. Oil on canvas, 46 × 36 in. (116.8 × 91.4 cm).

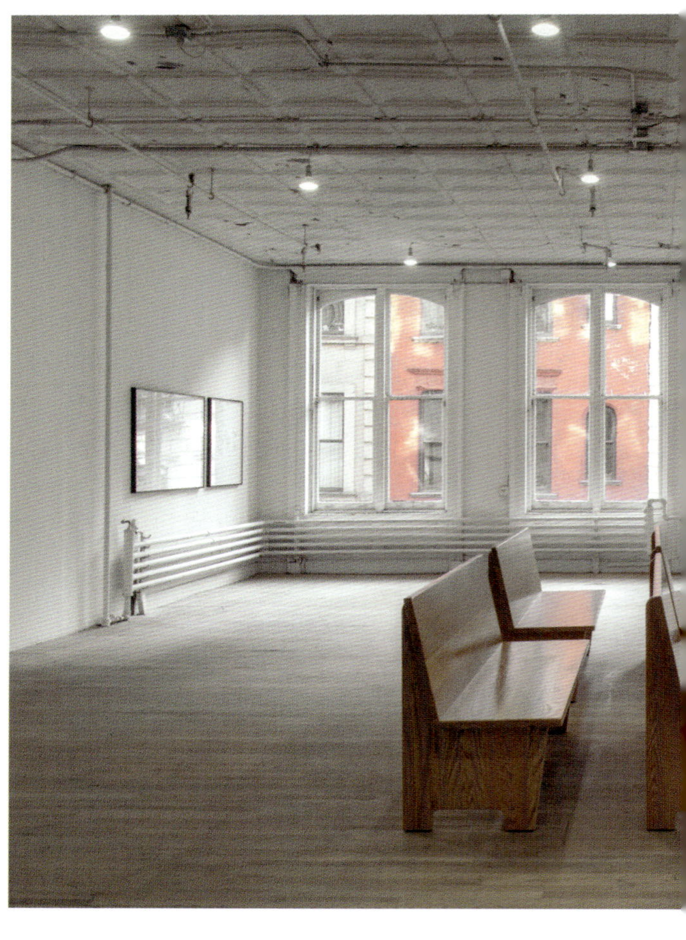

FIGURE 10. Cameron Rowland, *91020000*, 2016; installation view, Artists Space, New York.

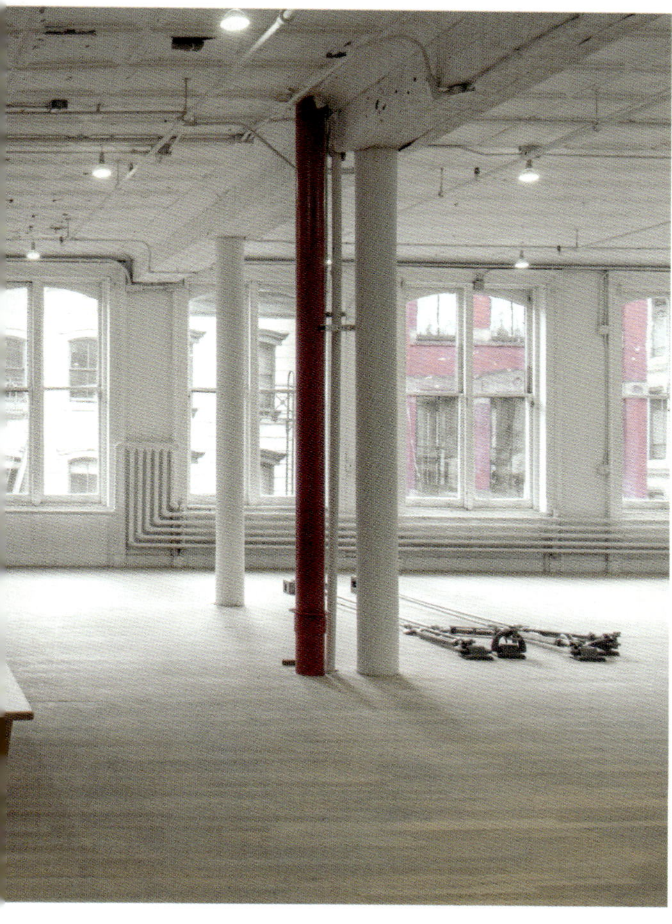

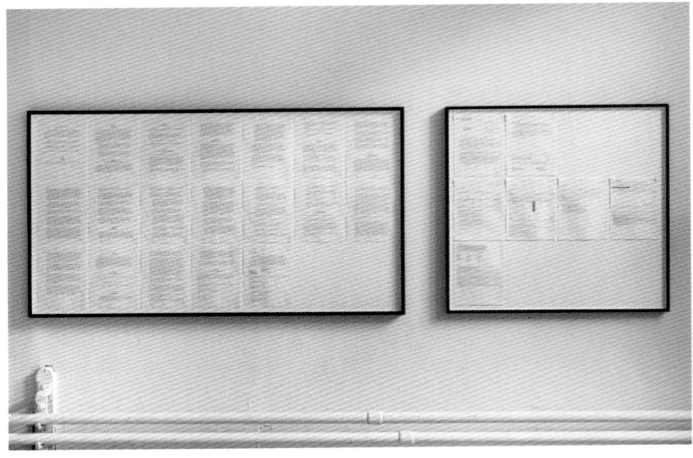

FIGURE 11. Cameron Rowland, *Disgorgement*, 2016. Reparations Purpose Trust, Aetna Shares.

Aetna, amongst other insurance companies, issued slave insurance policies, which combined property and life insurance. These policies were taken out by slave masters on the lives of slaves, and provided partial payments for damage to the slave and full payment for the death of the slave. Death or damage inflicted by the master could not be claimed. The profits incurred by these policies are still intact within Aetna.

In 1989 Congressman John Conyers of Michigan first introduced Congressional Bill H.R. 40, which would "Establish the Commission to Study Reparation Proposals for African Americans to examine slavery and discrimination in the colonies and the United States from 1619 to the present and recommend appropriate remedies." The bill would convene a research commission that would, among other responsibilities, make a recommendation as to whether a formal apology for slavery is owed, whether reparations are owed, what form reparations would then take and who would receive them. The bill has been reintroduced to every session of Congress since 1989. This bill acquired 48 cosponsors in 1999–2000. As of 2016 it has no cosponsors.

In 2000 the state of California passed the bill SB 2199, which required all insurance companies conducting business in the state of California to publish documentation of slave insurance policies that they or their parent companies had issued previously. In 2002 a lawyer named Deadria Farmer-Paellmann filed the first corporate reparations class-action lawsuit seeking disgorgement from 17 contemporary financial institutions including Aetna, Inc., which had profited from slavery. Farmer-Paellmann pursued property law claims on the basis that these institutions had been enriched unjustly by slaves who were neither compensated nor agreed to be uncompensated. Farmer-Paellman called for these profits and gains to be disgorged from these institutions to descendants of slaves.

The Reparations Purpose Trust forms a conditionality between the time of deferral and continued corporate growth. The general purpose of this trust is "to acquire and administer shares in Aetna, Inc. and to hold such shares until the effective date of any official action by any branch of the United States government to make financial reparations for slavery, including but not limited to the enactment and subsequent adoption of any recommendations pursuant to H.R. 40—Commission to Study Reparation Proposals for African-Americans Act." As a purpose trust registered in the state of Delaware this trust can last indefinitely and has no named beneficiaries.

The initial holdings of Reparations Purpose Trust consists of 90 Aetna shares. In the event that federal financial reparations are paid, the trust will terminate and its shares will be liquidated and granted to the federal agency charged with distributions as a corporate addendum to these payments. The grantor of the Reparations Purpose Trust is Artists Space, its trustee is Michael M. Gordon, and its enforcer is Cameron Rowland. The Reparations Purpose Trust gains tax-exemption from its grantor's nonprofit status.

MoMA has agreed to continue the trust if Artists Space is no longer able to serve as the grantor.

The Burden of Representation

Modern art is defined by the simultaneous entry of art's alterity into two distinct property regimes. The first depends upon the artwork's extraction from what Quatremère called its intended "purpose [*destination*]," or context. This preliminary physical alienation submits objects to exchange (whether through looting or commodification) and makes them available for curatorial recombination. Because modern art is characterized by the capture and curation of aesthetic forms of alterity, the museum, as Foucault argued long ago,[1] is the logical destination for modern art—its new locus of power. Coincident with the alienation and museumification of the artwork—its capture and curation—was its reconception as the representation of an artist's (and a nation's or community's) properties, or qualities. In this second regime of proprietary authorship, the temperament of an individual artist was made to represent *humanity in general* in variations on, or overrepresentations of, what Sylvia Wynter calls the figure of "Man." And, as I have argued, this form of proprietary authorship is profoundly racialized. Indeed, W.E.B. Du Bois's 1903 declaration that "the problem of the Twentieth Century is the problem of the color-line"[2] has proven as true in the realm of art as it has in society at large. This is because the value of self-possession varies dramatically according to one's race, gender, or ethnicity. If, for some, their personal properties function as an asset, for others they are a liability. In the 1900 Paris Exposition Universelle, Du Bois addressed racism by expanding the genre of the human to accommodate the properties of African American life. He did so by counteracting one aesthetic genre—the racist ethnography of the human zoo[3]—with two others: data visualization and photographic portraiture. Though I have no evidence that Du Bois's exhibition was conceived as a literal riposte to the displays of peoples from the Global South on exhibit nearby, it is significant that the two aesthetic approaches he pursued directly contravene the embodied "primitivism" of those installations. On the one hand, his ingenious, colorful, and engaging charts introduced an abstract language of social science, in which the human is understood as a statistical aggregate, and on the other, in the many photographic portraits included in *Nègres d'Amerique*, Black bodies were presented as individuals with all the markers of modern American sartorial style. Such a strategy of introducing or inventing alternative aesthetic genres of the human has been pursued throughout the twentieth century, from the painters associated with the Harlem Renaissance to the practitioners of Négritude, who as part of an anti-colonial and postcolonial movement embraced Africanness as an alternate modernity, to the Black Arts Movement of the 1960s, right through to Adrian Piper's transposition of Conceptual art's self-possession to a visceral performance of dispossession. It is my belief that such revisions of the "genre of the human" are what define a genuine avant-garde practice within modern art and that their radicality depends less on a particular formal practice—say abstraction or performance—than on a structural readjustment of what counts as human. In short, such practices challenge the imposition of possessive individualism as a pervasive modern ideology of which the artist has been a privileged representative. And indeed, such challenges to the nature of personhood as property are equally prevalent among white avant-gardists as they are with artists of color. The Dadaists, Surrealists, and Abstract Expressionists, to name only a few major tendencies of canonical Western modernism, were all dedicated to embodying a new experience of the human, a new genre of personhood outside of relations of property. As powerful as these efforts have been, they have also run up against the enduring, seemingly inescapable ideology of liberal self-possession and neoliberal entrepreneurship of the self. As I have argued, this occurs through the mechanism of representation, whereby, for instance, the Harlem Renaissance, as a category naming a multivalent array of singular practices, is made to stand in for Blackness in general. This is the danger of the museumification of difference or the compulsory projection of properties onto artists *as a form of property*, which Kobena Mercer has eloquently called "the burden of representation."[4]

It is to the politics of this unequally shared burden of representation that I will now turn, in assessing the controversy that resulted when Dana Schutz, a white New York painter, exhibited a work titled *Open Casket* (2016), which pictures the ravaged body of Emmett Till, a fourteen-year-old African American boy from Chicago savagely murdered by white supremacists while visiting relatives in Mississippi in 1955 (fig. 6). His "crime" was allegedly flirting with one of his assailant's wives. I will dwell on this case because the impassioned debates that erupted when *Open Casket* was included in the 2017 Whitney Biennial offer a particularly raw instance of art's contemporary economy of racialized property. I will have more to say about Till's brutal murder as it relates to what we might call the possessive gaze of Jim Crow America—a regulatory visual economy that controlled who could look at whom—and how the spectacle of lynching could function as a means of visual terror through its photographic dissemination. But for the moment, I will make just two points about the photographs of Till's body that served as the inspiration for Schutz's painting. First, it was Emmett's mother, Mamie Till-Mobley, who insisted that his funeral include an open casket and that his body be photographed and the photographs published in the Black press (later, the images were disseminated more widely and available to a broad multiethnic American and international public). But second, the photograph of Till's body is *excru-*

ciating to look at (fig. 7).[5] The violence done to him, including a beating about the head, the loss of his eyes, the destruction of his skull from a gunshot wound, and the bloating of his body resulting from its "disposal" in the Tallahatchie River after his death, render his visage monstrous. The image of this once-handsome child is literally made obscene, in that his murderers sought not only to take his life *but to obliterate his humanity* by destroying his face. This image of an atrocity sears the eyes of anyone who views it. In her devastating poem "Afterimages," in which she attempts to come to terms with the publicity of these photographs of Till as "a black child's mutilated body / fingered by street-corner eyes," Audre Lorde writes: "my eyes are caves, chunks of etched rock / tied to the ghost of a black boy / whistling."[6] It is an image, as Lorde suggests, that is etched in the eyes of those who see it.

The initial discursive salvo in the Schutz controversy was an open letter addressed to the biennial's curators, Christopher Y. Lew and Mia Locks, written by the Black British artist and writer Hannah Black and signed by several other Black artists, critics, and theorists. Black's eloquent riposte to Schutz's painting was expressed in explicitly proprietary terms, while marking an important juncture in the history of Blackness as property in the United States. Due to the continuous work of activists, artists, writers, theorists, and politicians, among others, "blackness," as Black put it, "is hot right now." In other words, on account of the success of Black Lives Matter (as a recent manifestation of a long history of civil rights struggles) and diverse forms of activism in the face of an epidemic of shootings of African Americans by police, the Black radical tradition came to be understood by many more white people on the left—and even many in the center politically—as an *asset*. After all, President Donald Trump's policies were explicitly founded on maintaining and strengthening white supremacy, so the long-standing analysis and political resistance of Black people offered effective tools of critique and resistance to Trumpism. But this reversal in valence (without, it must be said, a sufficient reversal in the actually existing conditions of systemic racism in the United States) made the appropriation of Black ideas and struggles attractive to white thinkers and artists. I must include myself and this book as part of such a phenomenon, but I hope to propose a concrete way of evaluating such allyship in the course of my analysis of the Schutz affair. For the moment, however, let's clarify the terms of the debate. Black's open letter introduces the question of property on two registers, which are closely imbricated in one another and in some ways even indistinguishable. First, she argues that Black pain is the exclusive property of Black people. Here is a long excerpt in the letter that suggests the tenor of proprietary pain as Black theorizes it:

> It is not acceptable for a white person to transmute Black suffering into profit and fun, though the practice has been normalized for a long time.

Although Schutz's intention may be to present white shame, this shame is not correctly represented as a painting of a dead Black boy by a white artist—those non-Black artists who sincerely wish to highlight the shameful nature of white violence should first of all stop treating Black pain as raw material. The subject matter is not Schutz's; white free speech and white creative freedom have been founded on the constraint of others, and are not natural rights.…

Emmett Till's name has circulated widely since his death. It has come to stand not only for Till himself but also for the mournability … of people marked as disposable, for the weight so often given to a white woman's word above a Black child's comfort or survival, and for the injustice of anti-Black legal systems. Through his mother's courage, Till was made available to Black people as an inspiration and warning. Non-Black people must accept that they will never embody and cannot understand this gesture: The evidence of their collective lack of understanding is that Black people go on dying at the hands of white supremacists, that Black communities go on living in desperate poverty not far from the museum where this valuable painting hangs, that Black children are still denied childhood.[7]

Black's fundamental point, that African Americans hold exclusive rights to the pain they experience, and have historically experienced, under conditions of systemic racism, is nuanced in subtle but significant ways. First, white shame (presumably a legitimate theme for white painters) should not use "Black pain as raw material." In other words, Schutz may have chosen an appropriate, even laudable, issue to address in *Open Casket*, but she failed to treat it properly, because she exploited the pain of others rather than exposing her own shame. In effect, Black suggests that Schutz attempted to proffer a political statement by appropriating the property of Black suffering as an *asset*, while concealing the liability of white shame as her own proprietary responsibility. Since there is little evidence of affective or thematic shame in the confident, even exuberant, rendering of *Open Casket*, the open letter implicitly recommends the redirection of Schutz's aesthetic focus from empathy for others to shame in oneself. Indeed, Black extends her profound critique of empathy by specifically limiting its efficacy to members of an ethnic group. Of Mamie Till-Mobley's circulation of the photographs of her son's funeral, Black states unequivocally: "Non-Black people must accept that they will never embody and cannot understand this gesture." Empathy from this perspective is an oppressive form of appropriation that moreover cannot be justified by recourse to free speech and creative freedom—which she declares are "not natural rights." Hence, the ideal of the emancipated artist, free to represent anything they wish, unconstrained by the strictures of censorship, is here explicitly racialized as a form of white privilege. The logical, if uncompromising corollary to the moral and legal illegitimacy of Schutz's appropriation of Black pain is plainly stated at the outset of the letter: "I am writing to ask you to remove Dana Schutz's painting *Open Casket* with the urgent recommendation that the painting be destroyed and not entered into any market or museum."[8]

The official response by both the Whitney and Schutz were premised on an understanding of the proprietary artist completely different from that of Black. In fact, it is hard to regard the affair as a genuine debate because there was no agreement on a shared set of terms. Instead, there was a collision of two incommensurable genres of the human, fracturing the paradigmatic figure of the self-possessed artist. Curators Lew and Locks published a short response in artnet.com that began as follows:

> The 2017 Whitney Biennial brings to light many facets of the human experience, including conditions that are painful or difficult to confront such as violence, racism, and death. Many artists in the exhibition push in on these issues, seeking empathetic connections in an especially divisive time. Dana Schutz's painting, *Open Casket* (2016), is an unsettling image that speaks to the long-standing violence that has been inflicted upon African Americans. For many African Americans in particular, this image has tremendous emotional resonance.[9]

The most obvious point at which the curators and Black diverge is in the former's celebration of "empathetic connections in an especially divisive time," implying that empathy *bridges* divisions without specifying how it can do this. Black is, of course, arguing that *empathy cannot bridge divisions*, and so, the curators fail to acknowledge Black's critique while doubling down on the museum's bland values of multicultural humanism. Lew and Locks are talking past Black, not with her, and their primary alibi is the "many facets of the human experience." In other words, the human—what Wynter called the overrepresentation of "Man" that incorporates all other genres of the human—absorbs the specificity of Blackness (as well as the specificity of every other race, ethnicity, gender, sexual expression, and so on). Lew returns to the universality of the human in an interview he gave to artnet.com. Here are a few of his statements:

> The violence [in works of art] is set within other aspects of the human condition and human experience—violence and death is there, but so is love, unity, self-preservation, and self-care.…
>
> If we do not see the humanity in one another, that's when we end up with divisions and barriers.

And regarding Schutz's painting, the question of empathy returns:

> They [speaking of *Open Casket* and Jordan Wolfson's 2017 virtual-reality work *Real Violence*] are both so woven into a dialogue about representation, about issues of violence that are both historical and contemporary, and about this idea of empathy—and these are all shared concerns across a diverse group of artists. They

are not concerns that are broken and divided by race. They are American concerns.[10]

In all these statements, Black's fundamental point—that Black pain is not the property of others or, in other words, that a generalized "humanity," traditionally coded as white and bourgeois throughout the entire history of modernity and modern art, *cannot* represent Black pain and cannot claim to possess it—is completely overlooked. Moreover, empathy returns as the perpetual alibi. In short, there is no real response to Black's critique, only a reversal of the valences of the two issues at stake: for Black, pain is the property of those who suffered it, or whose ancestors suffered it, and empathy cannot bridge the divisions of identity; for the curators, pain is the property of humanity, and empathy can bridge all divisions. There is no debate here, merely a kind of multicultural doublespeak, whose ostensible mildness masks its implicit invalidation of Black's perspective. This is the violence of the museumification of alterity, whose genealogy, as I have demonstrated, reaches back to Napoleon.

Schutz is a closer reader of the open letter than the curators, for she does engage with Black's critique of empathy. In a wall label accompanying *Open Casket* that addresses the controversy, Schutz states:

I did not know if I could make this painting, ethically or emotionally. It is easy for artists to self-censor, to convince yourself not to make something before even trying. I don't know what it is like to be Black in America. But I do know what it is like to be a mother. Emmett was Mamie Till-Mobley's only son. I thought about the possibility of painting it only after listening to interviews with her. In her sorrow and rage she wanted her son's death not just to be her pain but America's pain.

Schutz here makes two points that implicitly respond to Black's critique of empathy. Her first argument is that empathy may move across different subject positions—that while she is not Black, she can empathize with Mamie Till-Mobley as a mother. This argument has been rejected by several commentators on the grounds that the relation of motherhood for a Black woman in the 1950s is very different from that of a white woman in 2016. Ruth Feldstein has articulated the double bind Till-Mobley experienced in the trial of her son's murderers:

> Her authority as a mother challenged notions of good mothers as necessarily white, but it also relied on racial stereotypes that required Till[-Mobley] to be "humble" and upon gender stereotypes that required mothers to be overwrought. And the jury rejected even these conditional sources of power.[11]

The artist and critic Aria Dean is emphatic in her rejection of Schutz's empathetic identification: "The degree to which the murder of your child is incomprehensible to a white mother exists on a plane very distant from the way that possibility exists in the mind of a black mother. For the black mother, the possibility of violence and death for her black child is a reality, not a conceptual impossibility."[12] Despite the many ways that the experience of Black mothers is incommensurable with that of white ones, Schutz's understanding of empathy does not merely presume its universality, as Lew and Locks do in their statements. Instead, she opens a space of negotiation over how we might begin to know, or at least to care for and respect, the experiences of others. Schutz's second point is an important one—that Till-Mobley intended to share her pain with the entire country—and in fact the world. While this argument also met with criticism (it is true, for instance, that Till-Mobley intentionally had the photos of her son's funeral published in the Black press, leading some to argue that they were meant only for Black viewers),[13] I think the evidence clearly shows that his mother wished to have Emmett Till's story move well beyond the Black community, as it in fact did, and that she worked throughout her life to make that happen. If Schutz's claim to empathy through her experience as a mother suggests a mobile, even intersectional form of identification that can shift from opposing positions (Black vs. white) to analogous ones (shared love of a child), her reference to Till-Mobley's sustained effort to publicize Till's death introduces another approach. Here, one need not occupy any kind of analogous position with those who suffer pain as a prerequisite for identification with them. Till-Mobley, who was a devoted educator and whose teaching was inspired by her experiences of personal loss, might have called this approach pedagogical. It is clear from her memoir that she transposed her grief into an energetic and creative effort to tell Emmett Till's story in as many ways as she could and to as broad a public as possible. As flawed as Schutz's attempts at visual empathy may have been—and I will soon engage in an analysis of the painting itself—she understood that empathy requires an effortful translation of another's experience into one's own, rather than being an automatic or universal human responsiveness.

Perhaps the strongest reactions to Black's open letter were to her recommendation that *Open Casket* be destroyed. Many artists and critics, including people of color, likened this demand to book burning by the Nazis or the culture wars of the 1980s. In one of the most cogent and impassioned responses, the prominent artist and educator Coco Fusco wrote: "Presuming that calls for censorship and destruction constitute a legitimate response to perceived injustice leads us down a very dark path. Hannah Black and company are placing themselves on the wrong side of history, together with Phalangists who burned books, authoritarian regimes that censor culture and imprison artists, and religious fundamentalists who ban artworks in the name of their god."[14] Biennial curator Christopher Lew again ventriloquized the normative values of the museum, for which the work of art must be sanctified as an inviolable form of property. He declared, "To have a discussion around the destruction of an artwork is deeply problematic and disturbing—that's not something that we entertain as a museum."[15] Once more, Schutz's position is more nuanced, if equally problematic. She stages her choice of motif as a kind of moral necessity: "I did not know if I could make this painting, ethically or emotionally. It is easy for artists to self-censor, to convince yourself not to make something before even trying." In a profile in the *New Yorker*, Schutz pressed this point further by describing her choice to paint Emmett Till as a kind of obligation. Calvin Tomkins writes:

> "I knew the risks going into this," Schutz told me. "What I didn't realize was how bad it would look when seen out of context. Is it better to try to make something that's impossible, because it's important to you, and to fail, or never to engage with it at all? I just couldn't do it any other way."[16]

Here is a third model of empathy, or perhaps a proprietary perversion of empathy: the artist's self-appointed moral duty to appropriate a painful image that affects her deeply. Rather than confronting the proposed annihilation of her painting with the lessons of historic instances of censorship, as Fusco did, or respond like Lew, with an orthodox statement of museum values, which are dedicated to the perpetual conservation of objects, Schutz counters Black by describing her act of appropriation as a sacred duty—an avoidance of self-censorship (which, she states, would have been much easier than the risks of appropriation) in favor of the heroic attempt to possess the pain of Mamie Till-Mobley: "Is it better to try to make something that's impossible, because it's important to you, and to fail, or never to engage with it at all? I just couldn't do it any other way."

Hannah Black considers *Open Casket* obscene in its appropriation of African American pain, and she calls for the ultimate remedy when it comes to property—its destruction. Dana Schutz, on the other hand, sees it as her duty to appropriate those images that move her—in her view, the affective force she felt in seeing the photograph of Till's ravaged body and hearing his mother's story gives her the right to use them. Anything else, she declares, would lead to self-censorship. Although Black's and Schutz's positions seem irreconcilable, the critic Klaus Speidel has argued that, in actuality, they mirror one another ideologically, since each is rooted in a proprietary model of identity, or what he calls "representational segregation":

> By accepting that she cannot "own" the suffering of a black boy or a black woman but claiming ownership of the suffering of a mother [Schutz] accepts that ownership of subject-matter and group membership really *are* central to her painting's legitimacy. Rather than rejecting the idea of representational segregation, Schutz singles out her undeniable membership in a group, which she claims gives her the right to create new representations of the topic.[17]

I would add to Speidel's analysis that it is not only as a mother that Schutz makes claims of ownership of Till's image but also as an artist, whose moral obligation is to claim the pain of others as her own to represent. In this sense she subsumes the particularity of identity (as an African American, or as a mother) within a universal human right—the right of "Man," racially coded as white and epitomized by the figure of the artist—to appropriate all genres of the human. For several commentators, including Zadie Smith, the absurdity of promoting the exclusive ownership of Black pain is brought back to the proprietary act of representation. Smith's detailed response to Black's open letter pivots on the question of who may claim to legitimately represent Blackness (or by analogy any other identity). It is worth quoting her comments at length:

> I want to follow [Black's open] letter very precisely, along its own logic, in which natural rights are replaced by racial ones. I will apply it personally. If *I* were an artist, and if I could paint—could the subject matter [of Till's body in his casket] be mine? I am biracial. I have Afro-hair, my skin is brown, I am identified, by others and by myself, as a black woman. And if so, by the logic of the letter—if I understand it correctly—this question of subject matter, in my case, would not come up, as it would not come up for the author of the letter, Hannah Black, who also happens to be biracial and brown. Neither of us is American, but the author appears to speak confidently in defense of the African-American

experience, so I, like her, will assume a transnational unity.... Now I want to inch a step further. I turn from the painting to my children. Their beloved father is white, I am biracial, so by the old racial classifications of America, they are "quadroons." Could *they* take black suffering as a subject of their art, should they ever make any?[18]

Smith deftly deflates the proprietary claims of representation implicit in Black's open letter by invoking the fundamental instability of any act of representation. She confronts us with the question: Who is Black enough (and American enough) to represent African American pain? And this interrogative, like all questions of representation, metastasizes into ever finer distinctions: Does one need to have ancestors who were enslaved to legitimately empathize with Emmett Till? Would one have to have lived in the South? Do only fellow Black Chicagoans understand Mamie Till-Mobley's experience as an emigrant from Mississippi? Smith even hints at Black's lack of authority as a representative on her own terms, since she, like Smith herself, is biracial and not American. All of this is rhetorically effective, but ultimately it does little to undermine the ideology of self-possession that characterizes both Black's and Schutz's positions. Smith demonstrates the absurdity of the regime of proprietary representation—and effectively compares it with the equally arbitrary categories of antebellum racial classifications like the "quadroon"—without offering a real alternative. Ultimately, her perspective converges with Schutz's conviction that an artist's powerful affective response to an image qualifies her to appropriate it. The thorny problem at the heart of the controversy over *Open Casket*—that any act of inclusion entails a countervailing act of *exclusion*—remains unresolved. Property, under Western custom and law, remains a zero-sum game, and so, if African Americans own Black pain, others have no right to it, but if pain is the universal property of humanity, then no one has the right to exclude anyone else from appropriating it. If, for instance, one agrees with Black that Schutz had no right to appropriate Till's image, then one is left with the aporia articulated by Smith regarding who would constitute a legitimate representative of Blackness. Moreover, this perspective is premised on the imperative that each one of us must claim our properties and defend them from others. The world is consequently partitioned into heavily policed "reservations." But if one affirms the "universal" right of the artist to take whatever content they wish, then one risks obscuring the very real structural inequities between Black and white Americans. This "human right" is afforded to the genre of the human that Sylvia Wynter calls "Man," which, as we have seen, is built upon the marginalization of all but the white bourgeois subject. The enduring significance of the Schutz controversy is thus the clarity with which it manifests a constitutive impasse of modern and contemporary art at a moment of racial reckoning. For the proprietary model of art, which has characterized modernity since at least the late eighteenth century, is inadequate to address the white supremacy inherent in possessive individualism. The burden of representation, and corollary forms of multiculturalism that multiply the identities that are included in exhibitions or collections, will never lead us out of possessive individualism—the most such inclusion can do is to switch the valence of property in Blackness from a liability to an asset and thus make that newly attractive property even more susceptible to appropriation by white artists like Dana Schutz. If each of us regards our qualities as a form of property, then no genuine commonality is possible, since according to Western laws and norms, ownership is an exclusive right, one that precisely and quite literally is intended to *exclude.* How, then, can injustice be addressed without falling into "representational segregation" or "the burden of representation"? The only effective route is to exit the proprietary regime of possessive individualism.

Witness

From Napoleon's looting of artworks for his eponymous museum at the turn of the nineteenth century to the dynamic of capture and curation in contemporary museum selfies, modern and contemporary art has been politicized by a possessive gaze—a gaze whose power arises from the appropriation of art's alterity. The strategies of those who are dispossessed from this proprietary visual economy indicate a pathway out of it. Mamie Till-Mobley, for instance, who was robbed of her son, publicized her grief as a gift to the world. Contrary to both Hannah Black's and Dana Schutz's understanding of Till-Mobley as wielding a proprietary identity (as Black or as a mother, respectively), her management of Emmett's image was characterized by extraordinary generosity. By circulating photographs of his gruesomely damaged body, she allowed a broad public to *witness* her pain alongside her, rather than hoarding it as her own private property. The difference between a witness and a consumer lies in the former's responsibility to narrate their experience—one does not have to possess something to recount it, and crucially, a witness has an obligation to do justice to what they have seen, whereas a consumer is bound by no such moral exigency. A witness in court is obligated to tell the truth, but a proprietor has the right to dispose of their property however they wish. The legitimacy of a witness should never be established a priori based on their identity but, rather, should be judged upon the credibility of their testimony. Till-Mobley's intentional shaping of the reception of her dead son's image was a deeply political response to a double dispossession of African Americans under the conditions of white supremacism. On the one hand, since the period of slavery and during its Jim Crow aftermath, Black people had been forced into invisibility; on the other, conversely—and paradoxically—through stereotyping they were grotesquely spectacularized. Both forms of visual subjection—invisibility on the one hand and hypervisibility on the other—were intended to dehumanize African Americans. In the face of these conditions, Till-Mobley made Emmett's tragedy visible without allowing it to be recoded as a stereotypical allegory of toxic Black masculinity. Neither invisible nor stereotypical, Emmett's image was made available to be witnessed.

In her memoir, Till-Mobley recalls the advice she gave her son on the eve of his departure for Mississippi. Raised entirely in the North, Emmett had never experienced the racial "etiquette" of the South. His mother admonished: "If you're walking down the street and a white woman is walking toward you, step off the sidewalk, lower your head. Don't look her in the eye. Wait until she passes by, then get back on the sidewalk, keep going, don't look back."[1] In the end, Emmett did not remain invisible; he was noticed and regarded as a stereotypical threat by Carolyn Bryant, the white woman whose husband would be one of his murderers. bell hooks offers a historical and theoretical framework that contextualizes Till-Mobley's advice:

> One mark of oppression was that black folks were compelled to assume the mantle of invisibility, to erase all traces of their subjectivity during slavery and the long years of racial apartheid, so they could be better—less threatening servants. An effective strategy of white supremacist terror and dehumanization during slavery centered around white control of the black gaze. Black slaves, and later manumitted servants, could be brutally punished for looking, for appearing to observe the whites they were serving as only a subject can observe or see. To be fully an object was to lack the capacity to see or recognize reality. . . . Reduced to the machinery of bodily physical labor, black people learned to appear before whites as though they were zombies, cultivating the habit of casting the gaze downward so as not to appear uppity. To look directly was an assertion of subjectivity, equality. Safety resided in the pretense of invisibility.[2]

If invisibility could function as a form of safety for the enslaved (and later African Americans subjected to Jim Crow laws and vulnerable to lynching), it also was a means of shielding the violence of white assailants from punishment. In Mississippi, Emmett's body had been placed in a casket, and authorities intended to bury him (and the evidence of his murder) expeditiously. Till-Mobley demanded that the body be transported to Chicago, and upon its arrival there, she had the casket opened. Despite the trauma of confronting her son's viciously violated corpse, she fought against the forces that wanted to keep him invisible—as well as those who wished to give him visibility only as the stereotype of a predatory Black male. Her decision to have a public funeral and to publish photographs of the open casket were a means of integrating Emmett's corpse into an account—a narration—of his life.

And yet, Till-Mobley confronted another risk of dehumanization through her decision to publicize her son's death—that Emmett's individuality would be lost in the spectacular horror of the lynched body as an icon of white supremacist terror. Late nineteenth- and early twentieth-century lynchings were often raucous public events, sometimes advertised in advance and attended by large crowds of white spectators, men, women, and children alike. Although they often wished to make Black bodies invisible when alive, once Black subjects were rendered objects—corpses—their white antagonists often enhanced their visibility through photography. A press report of Thomas Brooks's 1915 lynching in Tennessee recounts the visual culture of the event:

> Hundreds of kodaks clicked all morning at the scene of the lynching. People in automobiles and carriages came from miles around to view the corpse dangling from the end of a rope.... Picture card photographers installed a portable printing plant at the bridge and reaped a harvest in selling postcards showing a photograph of the lynched Negro. Women and children were there by the score. At a number of country schools the day's routine was delayed until boy and girl pupils could get back from viewing the lynched man.[3]

This report demonstrates that lynchings were always intended to engage two distinct audiences: African Americans, whom they were meant to terrorize, and white attendees seeking a grotesque ritual affirmation of their pretense to racial superiority. Through her organization of a public funeral for Emmett, which was attended by thousands, and in her choice to allow the publication of photographs of her son's excruciatingly damaged body, Mamie Till-Mobley reframed the spectacle of lynching for both African American and white audiences. Instead of allowing Black pain to *represent* Blackness as a meaning to be consumed, Till-Mobley reintegrated her son's death back into Black life, not as its inevitable outcome but as a form of trauma to be witnessed—a trauma that could be repaired at least partially through the narration of Emmett's life. A crucial detail in this regard, which has been overlooked by virtually all the commentators on Schutz's *Open Casket*, are the three photographs that Till-Mobley mounted on the lining of the casket's raised lid, all picturing her son as a happy and handsome young man (fig. 8). These photographs individualize Emmett's story; they literally *give him back his face.* If he was killed for looking at Carolyn Bryant, and his eyes were brutally destroyed in the course of his murder, these snapshots remind mourners of a time when he had the capacity to see, the agency of an independent gaze. While the violence perpetrated upon him was undoubtedly experienced as a threat to some, if not all, of the Black people who attended his funeral or saw the published photographs of his open casket, it was simultaneously recoded as an opportunity to witness, narrate, and teach others that the violence inflicted upon Black people need not inevitably lead to social death. Rather than serving as fetishes of white supremacism, like the photographs and postcards of lynchings that were circulated among white communities who feared no reprisals for their actions, Mamie Till-Mobley brought images of lynching to a broader public and thus called upon Americans to witness the violence that Emmett and many other Black children and men and women had experienced and continue to experience. The response to these photographs helped to energize the Civil Rights Movement in the United States. Through creating a scene of witnessing, Emmett's mother politicized her son's death rather than claiming her grief as private property.

I believe that Till-Mobley's management of her son's image is much more generative than Hannah Black's critique of *Open Casket*, which is based on the principle of "representational segregation." Rather than trying to limit the circulation of his representation, Till-Mobley attempted to counter and recode how those images were *seen* or *witnessed*, by both white perpetrators and Black victims—and with a good deal of success. As hooks says, "An effective strategy of white supremacist terror and dehumanization during slavery centered around white control of the black gaze." Till-Mobley sought to regain control of this gaze, but that did not entail claiming Blackness as her private property. Throughout her life, Till-Mobley insisted that she must continue to tell her story—that as a witness to her son's degradation *she had a responsibility to narrate it*, rather than leaving the narration to white-controlled authorities. But never did she contend that this narration was her exclusive right or property. Rather than attempting to arrest the circulation of images of Black pain, she worked to pluralize its narration, to recount pain as a component of life rather than a death sentence. From this perspective, it is extremely significant that in her memoir, Till-Mobley began her story not with Emmett's murder but with his birth. For her, the way to narrate violence against African Americans was not to hoard it as property but rather to share it as a part of Black life—a *dimension* of her experience but never its totality. In this regard, I find the silence around Till-Mobley's prominent exhibition of three photographs of an ebullient Emmett on the lid of his open casket, and their absence from Schutz's *Open Casket*, enormously telling. Both Black and Schutz were intent on claiming Till as a representation of Black death, while his mother sought, instead, to insist on his tragedy as part of a Black life.

I dwell on Till-Mobley's strategic intelligence in shaping her son's photographic legacy because I believe it offers a way to evaluate Schutz's *Open Casket* without falling into a zero-sum tournament over the ownership of Black pain. Rather than adjudicating Schutz's right to represent Till's death, which only leads us back to the proprietary impasse inherent in possessive individualism, we may choose instead to evaluate how *Open Casket* bears witness to Till's lynching. To bear witness, as I have argued, requires recounting one's experience of an event, and so, as a first step, we need to analyze how *Open Casket* narrates the story of Emmett Till's death or, more specifically, Dana Schutz's encounter with the photographs from his funeral. But the mechanics of narration are inseparable from the ethics of a particular telling, and consequently, any artwork can be assessed only through the contingent judgments of each person who sees it. In other words, no narration can claim to be definitive (nor can it claim to be proprietary, as opposed to a representation where one thing stands in for another). Because the legitimacy of a narration is based on whether it is judged to be responsible to its subject, and because there will be many such judgments as well as many principles upon which to define responsibility, I believe it is by treating *Open Casket* as a narration that we may exit the double bind of possessive individualism, where either Black people have exclusive rights to Black life, or, alternatively, those rights are universal in a way that dispossesses African Americans from the specificity of their own experience under white supremacy. In short, we can judge and compare different ways of being responsible to a subject without suggesting a priori exclusions as Hannah Black and the signatories of her open letter do. A particular judgment may conclude that Schutz did not treat the excruciating theme she appropriated responsibly, but it will not disqualify her from doing so because she is white—nor will it indemnify Schutz from criticism on the grounds of her alleged "human right" to appropriate the experience of others under the banner of anti-censorship.

Open Casket is dominated by a closely framed image of Till's horizontal body, encompassing his torso and head. His legs are cropped out, at the right edge of the painting, and his head, resting on a golden pillow, nearly reaches the left edge. The oval of his face, whose disfigurement is indicated by layered, fluid marks in various shades of brown with highlights in black, white, red, and curdled green, rhymes with the shape and rendering of a red rose incongruously placed on the lower waist of the trousers. A similar set of marks is used to render the loose florets of the casket's lining, whose emphatic wide and plunging brushstrokes establish a band of whiteness bearing down on Emmett's body—a whiteness that may or may not allegorize racial whiteness. This body itself affords a strong contrast between Emmett's clothing—a crisp black suit and the relatively unmodulated plane of a bright white shirt—with the painterly slashing brushwork of Emmett's face. Typical of Schutz's art, there is a good deal of compression in this canvas, but it is nevertheless much more static than her sometimes manic compositions (including *Elevator* (2017), also exhibited in the biennial). The body is locked into place by a strong L-shaped formation established by the band of casket lining along the top of the canvas and the waistband of Emmett's suit at its right. Any evidence of arms is absent, so that the torso appears as a distinct shape joined to the head, which appears as though laid upon a golden platter. Undoubtedly, the relative blankness of the right three-fifths of the canvas led Schutz to balance Emmett's face with a romantic allegorical counterpart—the red rose—like a displaced broken heart. Both the rose and the circle of gold around Emmett's head, resembling a halo, endow the figure with a sanctified aura, but this effect is subtle, almost residual, rather than explicit, as in David Driskell's painting *Behold Thy Son* (1956), where Emmett is memorialized in a scene of crucifixion, in which his/Christ's figure is held around the waist by his mother/the Virgin Mary (fig. 9). (Significantly, in Driskell's painting, the composition of bold expressive brushstrokes delineating the head and body of the crucified figure may suggest physical aggression, but they do not attempt to represent Emmett's disfigurement mimetically.) It is possible, then, to see *Open Casket* as a portrait of a fallen saint, and yet, unlike Driskell's painting, Schutz's invites intimacy rather than the veneration called for by an altarpiece, which typically commands respect by keeping its viewers at a distance. On the contrary, the spectator is brought very close to Till in *Open Casket*, as though she were leaning almost directly over the open casket. This is a very different perspective from that of the mourners at Emmett's funeral, who naturally maintained a respectful distance from the body rather than bending over it to gape. But more important, *grief and horror* would have made such a close and sustained look enormously excruciating and socially awkward. It is very difficult to look at the photographs of Emmett's ravaged face, his skull brutalized, his lids closed over empty eye sockets. There are reports of mourners fainting at the sight of his corpse, and a famous photograph showing Mamie Till-Mobley convulsed with grief beside the casket gives an indication of how affective this sight was. Literary theorist Christina Sharpe captured some of this transgression when she asked, rhetorically, in a 2017 interview, "What white people looked into Emmett Till's casket? You see photographs of people lined up around the block to go into the church to view that open casket, people fainting. There were no white people there. So this is a question of intimacy. What is the relation to the Black brutalized body? The painter assumes an intimate relation to it. The viewer is put in intimate relation to it. Are those the same intimate relations?"[4] By making Till's body intimately available to an anonymous viewer (ourselves in 2017, in the Whitney galleries) and by allowing us to press our noses against the glass cover of the coffin, while simultaneously making the painting so benign and even ingratiating—by formally rhyming the mangled flesh of a fourteen-year-old lynching victim with the lush petals of a rose—Schutz, I believe, fails to responsibly bear witness to the horror of her subject. Instead, she invites us (and by *us*, I mean the white viewers, among whom I include myself) to consume this image of terror and trauma without having to feel the revulsion, anger, and shame that her photographic sources inspire. Schutz's remarks to Calvin Tomkins in the *New Yorker* profile, which was being prepared before the biennial but was published after the controversy unfolded, clearly articulate the formal transposition of horror into benign empathy encoded in the painting:

In the current climate of political and racial unrest, Emmett Till seemed like a risky subject for a white artist to engage with. "I've wanted to do a painting for a while now, but I haven't figured out how," she said. "It's a real event, and it's violence. But it has to be tender, and also about how it's been for his mother." ... In a later conversation she said, "How do you make a painting about this and not have it just be about the grotesque? I was interested because it's something that keeps on happening. I feel somehow that it's an American image."[5]

I think the ethical offense in Schutz's painting is that she sought to make something that is insufferably grotesque—the brutal evidence of white supremacy that seared itself on the eyes of a generation—into something not "just . . . about the grotesque." She wished to render Mamie Till-Mobley's enormous courage in withstanding the degradation of her brutally murdered son, and the additional humiliation of his murderers' trial, in which her testimony as a *witness*—her identification of Emmett's body—was blithely disqualified, in a gross miscarriage of justice, as something "tender." It is indisputable that Till-Mobley had deeply tender private feelings for her son—these were indexed by the photographs that were fixed to the lid of the coffin, which do not appear in *Open Casket*—but the feelings she had for his corpse were outrage and a passionate desire to gain justice for Emmett, to bear witness to his death in a way that would draw attention, not to her private loss or her tender feelings but to systemic racism in the United States. *Open Casket* domesticates the horror of Emmett Till's death while simultaneously privatizing Mamie Till-Mobley's grief by making a painting that invites an unearned intimacy. *Open Casket* allows viewers to come too close to something horrible, without having to encounter anything too "grotesque." Schutz forecloses the public nature of Till-Mobley's motherhood— the way she endured the publicity of her grief not as "tender" but rather as an ethical and political demand. Rather than bearing witness to Till-Mobley's political and social project, Schutz reprivatizes Till's tragedy as a mother's personal loss; in other words, she reappropriates Till-Mobley's generosity in sharing her son's legacy with the world as a form of possessive individualism exercised first (in Schutz's view) by Till-Mobley as a mother and then reappropriated by herself as an artist who is a mother. It is the privatization of Till-Mobley's political project, the transposition of systemic racism into a personal tragedy, and the abdication on behalf of its viewers of any responsibility for their intimate encounter with the image of Emmett's corpse that makes *Open Casket* obscene, not the fact that it was painted by a white woman.

Mamie Till-Mobley transposed her experience of personal dispossession into a visual statement of dis-possession—a literal refusal of possessive individualism. Her method for doing so was to replace the possessive gaze of a spectator-consumer with a viewer's responsibility to narrate, or bear witness, to what she has seen. Through his mother's generosity, Emmett's sacrifice was literally dis-possessed, in that Till-Mobley no longer claimed to own it (but only after wresting control of his body and his story from authorities in the State of Mississippi). Both Hannah Black's and Dana Schutz's responses to Till-Mobley's radical gesture were reactionary, in that they reappropriated her experience as property. For Black, Till's pain and sacrifice were claimed as the property of Black people; for Schutz his death was offered up to (white) viewers as a consumable private experience of empathy—of tenderness—that, in the painter's view, mirrored Till-Mobley's equally personal experience as a mother. The reason I have dwelled on what might be considered a passing controversy is that it registers a contemporary crisis in the property regime of modern art. As different as their perspectives seem to be, *both* Black and Schutz had phobic reactions to Till-Mobley's embrace of dis-possession as a political strategy; both, from their different perspectives, called for a reinstatement of the proprietary regime of "representational segregation" that Till-Mobley's actions had threatened. What this shows us, as Klaus Speidel had recognized, is that the *Open Casket* affair exacerbates the conflict inherent in possessive individualism—the zero-sum game of the private property vested in identity—without showing us a way out of its double bind. Art's regime of property will not be dismantled by proprietary counterclaims such as those made in Black's open letter or Schutz's and her defenders' cries of censorship. As I have indicated in my account of modern art's constituent procedures of alienation and appropriation, its proprietary regime is founded on principles of racialized representation and regulation that undergird white supremacy. In order to dismantle ideologies of proprietary identity, it is necessary, as Till-Mobley understood, to embrace and recode dispossession as a form of dis-possession.

Narration is the strategy of the witness, and as such, a careful consideration of its qualities will help us to differentiate between the figure of the witness as a "genre of the human" and the hegemonic figure of "Man" as defined by Sylvia Wynter. In her book *Relating Narratives*, Adriana Cavarero distinguishes between a philosophical mode of questioning that tends to the universal—to Man—versus narrative perspective, which embodies singularity. She writes:

> We could define it as the confrontation between two distinct registers that manifest opposite characteristics. One, that of philosophy, has the form of a definitory knowledge that regards the universality of Man. The other, that of narration, has the form of a biographical knowledge that regards the unrepeatable identity of someone. The questions that sustain the two discursive styles are equally diverse. The first asks, "*what* is Man?" The second asks instead of someone "*who* he or she is."[6]

I would further specify that the philosophical perspective, as defined by Cavarero, corresponds to a visual and interpretive regime of representation where a term or image stands for a concept or meaning in a one-to-one relationship. In the course of this book, I have argued that representation is a tool of possessive individualism, the product of a proprietary gaze. Narrative, on the other hand, is constitutively plural, and unlike a philosophical truth, it cannot be refuted—but, importantly, it can be submitted to ethical judgment in a way that universal concepts cannot. In this regard, a narrative approach to the production and interpretation of art is better suited to encompassing its alterity, defined as its capacity to produce infinite readings, infinite narratives. This would mean that the chaining of images to an implicit philosophical universality, as a predominant contemporary tradition of modernist art history has done, risks foreclosing art's alterity. Representation encloses alterity to produce power; narrative instantiates alterity to make it accessible for ethical encounters and judgments. Cavarero dwells on a passage from Hannah Arendt's discussion of the writer Isak Dinesen:

> It is true that storytelling reveals meaning without committing the error of defining it, that it brings about consent and reconciliation of things as they really are, and that we may even trust it to contain eventually by implication that last word which we expect from the "day of judgment."[7]

Arendt's extraordinary characterization of storytelling as "reveal[ing] meaning without committing the error of defining it" is a pithy encapsulation of the politics of dis-possession as expertly practiced by Mamie Till-Mobley. Social justice requires that meanings proliferate, but they must cease to be enclosed as private property. Their freedom is crucial because, as Cavarero argues, "The existent is the exposable *and* the narratable; neither exposability nor narratability, which together constitute this peculiarly human uniqueness, can be taken away. The one who is exposed generates and is generated by the life-story."[8] In other words, the capacity to narrate one's life is what defines—and can *redefine*—the human. Narration is the praxis of dis-possession.

The Object as Witness

A progressive politics of art must embrace dis-possession. During the nineteenth and early twentieth centuries, the modern artist, as the sole proprietor of an aesthetic sensibility and its singular products, was an exemplary figure of liberal possessive individualism, and since the mid-twentieth century, the figure of the artist—or "the creative"—has exemplified neoliberal entrepreneurship of the self. In the first phase of modern art in Europe and its diaspora, roughly spanning 1790–1960, an artist's principal property was their style. Within the developing dealer-critic system, this singular style brought them notoriety, which was necessary if not sufficient for financial and reputational success. The avant-gardes of the early and mid-twentieth century intensified emphasis on a proprietary style while simultaneously experimenting with various forms of revolutionary dis-possession. Indeed, the contradictions between modern European diaspora art's embrace of a politics of dis-possession, in for instance, the Constructivists' or Surrealists' distinct revolutionary projects, versus the art market's capacity to commodify both styles and artworks, is one of the central paradoxes animating modernist art history. Later, in a subsequent phase of modern art, initiated by the emergence of Conceptual art as an identifiable tendency at the end of the 1960s,[1] art's property conformed more closely to a neo-liberal regime in which the artist is valued for their innovative development of intellectual property rather than their aesthetic facility or style. The proprietary regime of modernism has never, of course, been monolithic, and individual artists have always found ways to resist—especially, as we have seen, those cognizant of or subjected to conditions of dispossession. In its emphasis on text over a contingent or "dematerialized" object, Conceptual art opened out to multiple forms of narration. And indeed, as the differences I have noted between Lawrence Weiner's and Adrian Piper's works demonstrate, the dynamic in Conceptual art—its authorization of anything whatsoever as art once an author's name has been attached to it—allows for a wide spectrum of proprietary claims, ranging from Weiner's assertion of an authoritative intention that would take precedence over any single manifestation of one of his works to Piper's delegation of the narration of her actions in *Catalysis* to random passersby who happened to witness them. In other words, the proprietary regime of Conceptual art—and of modern art in general, which it epitomizes—could accommodate the challenges of Piper's extreme act of dis-possession as well as those of many artists since.

In recent years, Cameron Rowland has brought Conceptual art's capacity to politicize dis-possession to a breaking point. He applies the categorical disruption pioneered in Marcel Duchamp's readymades to the legacy of the enslaved—the human-as-property. In projects like the exhibition *91020000*, which took place at Artists Space in New York in 2016 (fig. 10), Rowland builds on the work of prominent historians to explore how slavery persists in the conditions of contemporary prisons (whose population in the United States is disproportionately African American). In his deeply researched essay published in a free booklet accompanying the exhibition, Rowland argues that this legacy pivots on a continuous, if transformed, practice of forced labor, whose legal object, as set forth in the Thirteenth Amendment of the US Constitution (ratified in 1865), shifted from the enslaved to prisoners: "Neither slavery nor involuntary servitude, except as a punishment for crime whereof the party shall have been duly convicted, shall exist within the United States, or any place subject to their jurisdiction."[2] In *91020000*, Rowland links these two phases of involuntary servitude with two distinct aesthetic formats: the readymade and the legal trust. Readymade objects such as an L-shaped desk, levelers for manhole openings, wooden benches intended for courtrooms, and Nomex fire-retardant suits, all produced by prison laborers at minuscule wages to be distributed to state agencies and registered nonprofit organizations (like Artists Space), constituted the preponderance of the exhibition.[3] Unlike

Duchamp's readymades, which reversed or exchanged the designation of the ordinary commodity and the artwork, Rowland exchanges the categories of free and forced labor by causing a viewer to realize that what seem to be ordinary commodities are in fact generated in a carceral market of coercion.[4] Instead of profit, the products of inmates, as Rowland argues in his essay, lead to *savings* by the state: "These savings, as absences of costs or information, operate as financial and rhetorical instruments of governmental opacity." Rowland's readymades illuminate a double opacity or invisibility: the persistence of forced labor among prisoners as a legacy of slavery, and the state's profiting from this labor. As a second device alongside the readymade, Rowland uses the legal trust as a monumental form—an instrument whose very purpose is to persist through time. The 2016 work *Disgorgement* (fig. 11) adopts the format of a Reparations Purpose Trust that holds ninety shares in Aetna, one of many insurance companies to have profited historically from insuring the enslaved. Rowland explains that only if "federal financial reparations are paid, the trust will terminate and its shares will be liquidated and granted to the federal agency charged with distribution."[5] Although *Disgorgement* itself is not visually imposing, it is nonetheless literally a monument that will bear witness over time to the American government's refusal to acknowledge the economic, psychological, and physical violence of slavery and its legacy in the United States. *Disgorgement* is thus doubly a monument to dispossession: it marks the absence of reparations and the physical absence of the enslaved who died or were thrown overboard during their passage and whose lives were commemorated only as a business loss.[6] Rowland's linking of slavery and prison labor underlines an important theoretical dimension of the readymade—that objectification is a historical process rather than a punctual event (i.e., the transformation, for instance, of urinal to sculpture in Duchamp's *Fountain* of 1917). Forcing a person to become a thing, Rowland shows us, results from a sustained and effortful program of white supremacy, whose evidence, while often opaque, surrounds us in our everyday lives.

Perhaps Rowland's most notorious gesture of dispossession in *91020000* is his decision to sell only a proportion of his works, while offering others for rent at cost through a complex and carefully considered contractual agreement.[7] On the one hand, this arrangement objectifies the artist by placing him in the disadvantaged economic position of a prison laborer. But it simultaneously dispossesses his potential collectors by denying those who choose to rent both the exclusive right of ownership and its corollary benefit of the artwork's anticipated appreciation over time. Rowland thus systematically submits every element of art's production and display to dis-possession: the artwork, the artist, and the private or institutional collector. But as significant as this critique of modern art's proprietary regime is, it points to a broader aesthetic goal: to transform the art object into a witness. Despite what might sound like a dry assortment of things, *91020000* was an affectively exciting and invigorating show; its components were strategically placed to create a complex alternation of material densities and spatial voids within Artists Space's loft-like gallery. Rowland's disposition of objects, reanimated in ways unrelated to their designated function, presented a challenge to viewers: Why does this ordinary stuff seem so lively? What is its story? And indeed, as I have argued, this is the fundamental question guiding a politics of dis-possession: *What is your story?* These objects face the viewer like a chorus; Rowland's booklet gives them their voice. Without this text, few visitors would know that the steel desk was made by prisoners at the Attica Correctional Facility or that the oak benches were made at Green Haven Correctional Facility. These objects *dare* us to learn what they are witnesses to—the prisoners who are forced to furnish the very courtrooms where they were sentenced, the enslaved who were lost at sea. These objects refuse to represent (that is why they are placed out of context). They are freed from their normative function in order to bear witness. To encounter them is to learn to listen for their stories.[8]

Afterword

Dis-possession can be liberating only if it constitutes an exit from possessive individualism. The dispossession of the enslaved and colonial subjects, in contrast, was due not to exclusion but rather to their *inclusion* within a modern proprietary system as not-quite-humans or nonhumans.[1] *Dis-possession* in hyphenated form is a state in which no person—whether colonizer or colonized, slaveholder or enslaved—can deploy themselves, or others, as a form of property. Dis-possession arises from contact with the fundamental alterity of life, a force that ultimately resists appropriation or representation. Art brings such alterity into the world, and therein lies its paradox. No one can deny that artworks exhibit properties and are subject to exchange as real property, but in their temporal infinitude—their alterity—they can never be fully consumed. The modern politics of art, however, attempts to do just that—to capture art's alterity as a form of private property. These politics are not *in* art but around it. The dis-possessed spectator (a category that includes artists themselves) may counter such acts of capture and curation by witnessing rather than accumulating artworks as cultural or financial capital. Witnessing is the antithesis of possessing—its radical generosity opens a field of ethical contestation. The witness is a figure of dis-possession because she bears responsibility to what she sees rather than defending her exclusive rights to it. Witnesses hold no exclusive rights; their narratives are multiple but always subject to a political process of evaluation and verification. They are accountable not only to themselves but to the world.

Acknowledgments

This short book is a long postscript, a continuation, of conversations that took place in my Fall 2020 seminar, "From Biopolitics to Care of the Self," at Harvard. I am enormously grateful for the intellectual generosity and brilliance of the graduate students in that class: Max Bowens, Yongyu Chen, Yufan Chen, Mattlyn Córdova, Aaron Gluck-Thaler, Keisha Knight, Julia Sharpe, Anna Vichkitova, Valerie Werder, and Shaowen Zhang. *Art's Properties* is dedicated to them. I was ably assisted in preparing the manuscript by three equally outstanding PhD candidates. Caufield Schnug conducted research with ingenuity and alacrity; Nace Zavrl managed the difficult task of acquiring photo rights and reproductions with great professionalism; and Paul Chouchana checked my translations from the French. Colleagues Ewa Lajer-Burcharth, Neil Levine, and Tom Conley generously offered advice on specific topics, while two anonymous readers for Princeton University Press gave me valuable feedback, much of which I've acted on. I am grateful for the early and continuing support of Michelle Komie, Publisher for Art and Architecture at the Press, as well as the expert management of Kenneth Guay, Art Publications Coordinator. I feel a special debt of gratitude to Cameron Rowland, whose work introduced me to many of the questions around property that I explore here. *Art's Properties* was written entirely during the pandemic, in the company of Steve and Joey. I thank them for providing a silver lining to the lockdown through their love and companionship.

Notes

Prologue

Benjamin Krusling, from "I Will Live with Intent Not Glaring and Ripping," in Benjamin Krusling, *Glaring* (Brooklyn: Wendy's Subway, 2020), p. 36.

1. Depot Boijmans Van Beuningen, accessed March 15, 2021, https://www.boijmans.nl/en/depot.

2. The Broad, "About: The Building," accessed March 15, 2021, https://www.thebroad.org/about/building.

3. See Ruha Benjamin, *Race after Technology: Abolitionist Tools for the New Jim Code* (Cambridge, UK, and Medford, MA: Polity, 2019); and Safiya Umoja Noble, *Algorithms of Oppression* (New York: NYU Press, 2018).

4. Alice Morby, "The Broad Imposes a 30-Second 'Selfie Rule' at Yayoi Kusama Exhibition," Dezeen, October 24, 2017, accessed March 15, 2021, https://www.dezeen.com/2017/10/24/yayoi-kusama-imposes-30-second-selfie-rule-on-visitors-infinity-mirrors-exhibition-news/. As of early 2022, according to the Broad's website, these times have been revised; it advises: "You can view *Infinity Mirrored Room—The Souls of Millions of Light Years Away* (2013) for up to 1 minute and *Longing for Eternity* (2017) for about 45 seconds. Same day re-entry is not allowed." The Broad, accessed January 5, 2022, https://www.thebroad.org/art/yayoi-kusama/infinity-mirrored-room-souls-millions-light-years-away.

5. For another account of art as a form of currency, see my *After Art* (Princeton, NJ: Princeton University Press, 2013).

6. See Walter Benjamin, "The Work of Art in the Age of Its Technological Reproducibility," (2nd version), in Walter Benjamin, *Selected Writings*, vol. 3, *1935–1938*, ed. Howard Eiland and Michael W. Jennings; trans. Edmund Jephcott, Howard Eiland, et al. (Cambridge, MA: Belknap Press of Harvard University Press, 2002), pp. 101–33.

7. Hito Steyerl, Coco Fusco, Raqs Media Collective, and Supercommunity, "Remembering Okwui Enwezor," *e-flux journal* 98 (March 2019), p. 7, accessed March 11, 2021, https://www.e-flux.com/journal/98/260819/remembering-okwui-enwezor/.

8. For a brilliant methodological approach to understanding images as durational, see Tina Campt, *Listening to Images* (Durham, NC: Duke University Press, 2017).

9. Christopher S. Wood, *A History of Art History* (Princeton, NJ: Princeton University Press, 2019), pp. 133, 126, 404.

Alienability and Alterity

1. Henri Focillon, *The Life of Forms in Art*, trans. Charles B. Hogan and George Kubler (New York: Zone Books, 1989 [originally published in French as *La vie des forms*, 1934]), p. 154.

2. For a powerful argument with regard to how revolutionary politics can reanimate the past as a means of creating new futures through insurgency, see Massimiliano Tomba, *Insurgent Universality: An Alternative Legacy of Modernity* (New York: Oxford University Press, 2019).

3. Marie-José Mondzain, *Image, Icon, Economy: The Byzantine Origins of the Contemporary Imaginary*, trans. Rico Franses (Stanford, CA: Stanford University Press, 2005) [originally published in French as *Image, Icône, Économie: Les sources Byzantines de l'imaginaire contemporain*, 1996], p. 101.

4. Ibid., p. 176.

5. There is an echo here of Ernst H. Kantorowicz's classic account of medieval political theory, *The King's Two Bodies: A Study in Medieval Political Theology*, with a new introduction by Conrad Leyser and a preface by William Chester Jordan (Princeton, NJ: Princeton University Press, 2016 [originally published in 1957]). There is the physical

body of the king, which is mortal, and the sacred role of king, which
is immortal.

6. Jean-Paul Sartre, *The Imaginary: A Phenomenological Psychology of the Imagination* (London: Routledge, 2004 [originally published in French as *L'Imaginaire*, 1940]), p. 20.

7. Ibid., p. 9.

8. Ibid., pp. 189–90.

Constituent Moments: 1793-1815

1. Jason Frank, *Constituent Moments: Enacting the People in Postrevolutionary America* (Durham, NC: Duke University Press, 2010), p. 8.

2. Ibid., p. 245.

3. Andrew McClellan, *Inventing the Louvre: Art, Politics, and the Origins of the Modern Museum in Eighteenth-Century Paris* (Berkeley: University of California Press, 1994), p. 96.

4. Quoted in Ibid.

5. Isabelle Leroy-Jay Lemaistre, "Le Musée du Louvre," in Sylvain Laveissière, *Napoléon et le Louvre* (Paris: Musée du Louvre, 2004), p. 193 (my translation).

6. Wood, *A History of Art History*, p. 176.

7. Cecil Gould, *Trophy of Conquest: The Musée Napoléon and the Creation of the Louvre* (London: Faber and Faber, 1965), p. 90.

8. Sylvain Laveissière, "Introduction," in Laveissière, *Napoléon et le Louvre*, p. 9 (my translation).

9. Quoted in Isabelle Leroy-Jay Lemaistre, "Le Musée des Monuments Français," in Laveissière, *Napoléon et le Louvre*, p. 202 (my translation).

10. Quoted in Dominique Poulot, "Alexandre Lenoir et les musées des monuments français," in Pierre Nora, ed., *Les Lieux de mémoire*, vol. 1 (Paris: Éditions Gallimard, 1997), p. 1535 (my translation).

11. See Gould, *Trophy of Conquest*, p. 118.

12. For Canova's diplomatic mission, see Christopher M.S. Johns, "'This Great Cavern of Stolen Goods': Canova and the Repatriation of the Papal Collections from Paris in 1815," in *Antonio Canova and the Politics of Patronage in Revolutionary and Napoleonic Europe* (Berkeley:

University of California Press, 1998), pp. 171–94; and also, for an account of Canova in the context of the period more generally, see Thomas Crow, *Restoration: The Fall of Napoleon in the Course of European Art, 1812–1820* (Princeton, NJ: Princeton University Press, 2018).

13. M. Quatremère de Quincy, *Considérations Morales sur la destination des ouvrages de l'art; ou, De l'Influence de leur emploi sur le génie et le goût de ceux qui les produisent ou qui les jugent, et sur le sentiment de ceux qui en jouissent et en reçoivent les impressions* (Paris: L'Imprimerie de Crapelet, 1815), pp. 56–57 (my translation).

14. Ibid., p. 57–58 (my translation).

15. Dan Hicks, *The Brutish Museum: The Benin Bronzes, Colonial Violence and Cultural Restitution* (London: Pluto Press, 2020).

16. Aimé Césaire, *Discourse on Colonialism*, trans. Joan Pinkham (New York: Monthly Review Press, 1972 [originally published in French as *Discours sur le colonialisme*, 1955]), p. 71.

17. Ibid., p. 36.

18. Undoubtedly, Napoleon did intend to expand his efforts beyond Europe. As part of his unsuccessful—some would say disastrous—campaign in Egypt, he established the Institut d'Égypt, which remains to this day an important scholarly center. It is certain that its project of studying Egyptian history and culture would have led to a large influx of objects into the Louvre. As it happened, only a small number were brought to Paris as part of this campaign. See Thierry Lentz, "Napoléon, les Arts, la Politique," in Laveissière, *Napoléon et le Louvre*, pp. 16–21.

19. Ibid., p. 42.

20. For an important account of museums and governmentality, see Tony Bennett, *The Birth of the Museum: History, Theory, Politics* (London: Routledge, 1995), especially chapter 2, "The Exhibitionary Complex," pp. 59–88.

21. Mahmood Mamdani, *Define and Rule: Native as Political Identity* (Cambridge, MA: Harvard University Press, 2012), p. 2.

22. Mahmood Mamdani, *Neither Settler nor Native: The Making and Unmaking of Permanent Minorities* (Cambridge, MA: Belknap Press of Harvard University Press, 2020), p. 2.

23. Ibid., p. 4.

24. Ibid., p. 41.

25. Ibid., p. 65.

26. See Saloni Mathur and Kavita Singh, eds., *No Touching, No Spitting, No Praying: The Museum in South Asia* (London: Routledge, 2015); and my *Heritage and Debt: Art in Globalization* (Cambridge, MA: October Books, MIT Press, 2020).

27. Interestingly, though, later in the nineteenth century, as an outgrowth of the Paris Exposition Universelle of 1878, at the initiative of architect and theorist of restoration Eugène Viollet-le-Duc, the Musée de Sculpture Comparée was established in 1882 to exhibit plaster casts of medieval French architecture. In 1937 it was renamed the Musée des Monuments Français, which in 2007 became part of La Cité de l'Architecture et du Patrimoine. The Musée de Cluny in Paris, dedicated to French art from antiquity to the Renaissance, was founded in 1843 when an important private collection was acquired by the French state and housed in a building that includes an excavation of Gallo-Roman baths. The Cluny was partly inspired by Lenoir's Musée des Monuments Français, but like the later plaster-cast museum that bears that name, it emerged in a period when French feudal history had been firmly and "safely" historicized.

28. For a detailed account of Lenoir's installation, see chapter 5, "Alexandre Lenoir and the Museum of French Monuments," in McClellan, *Inventing the Louvre*, pp. 155–97.

29. Thierry Lentz, "Napoléon, les Arts, la Politique," in Laveissière, *Napoléon et le Louvre*, p. 27 (my translation).

Modern Art Was Always Conceptual

1. Quoted in Katie Scott, *Becoming Property: Art, Theory and Law in Early Modern France* (New Haven, CT: Yale University Press, 2018), p. 281. For the full text of the 1793 act, see *Décret de la Convention Nationale du 19 Juillet 1793. . . . relatif aux droits de propriété des auteurs d'écrits en tout genre, des compositeurs de musique, des peintres et dessinateurs*, Internet Archive, accessed April 28, 2021, https://archive.org/details/dcretdelaconvent00fran_3/mode/2up.

2. For good introductions to the history of copyright, see Mark Rose, *Authors and Owners: The Invention of Copyright* (Cambridge, MA: Harvard University Press, 1993); Elena Cooper, *Art and Modern Copyright* (Cambridge: Cambridge University Press, 2018); Martha

Woodmansee, *The Author, Art, and the Market: Rereading the History of Aesthetics* (New York: Columbia University Press, 1994).

3. Harrison C. and Cynthia A. White, *Canvases and Careers: Institutional Change in the French Painting World*, with a new foreword and afterword (Chicago: University of Chicago Press, 1993 [originally published in 1965]), p. 88.

4. Ibid., p. 98.

5. Scott, *Becoming Property*, p. 287. See also pp. 281–96.

6. Mark Rose, *Authors and Owners*, p. 129. See also, Mark Rose, "The Technology of Copyright in 1735: The Engraver's Act," *Information Society* 21: 1, 63–66.

7. Of course, this took a long time to happen, precisely because a feminine identity during this period (and until today in many ways) was, for an artist, a property that was a form of liability.

8. See Peter Osborne, *Anywhere or Not at All: Philosophy of Contemporary Art* (London: Verso, 2013).

9. This was already the strategy of Marcel Duchamp in his practice of the readymade in 1913–15 and beyond.

10. Michel Foucault, *The Birth of Biopolitics: Lectures at the Collège de France, 1978–1979*, ed. Michel Senellart, trans. Graham Burchell (New York: Palgrave Macmillan, 2008) [originally published in French as *Naissance de la Biopolitique: Cours au Collège de France, 1978–1979*, 2004], p. 226.

11. C. B. Macpherson, *The Political Theory of Possessive Individualism: Hobbes to Locke*, with a new introduction by Frank Cunningham (Oxford: Oxford University Press, 2011 [originally published in 1962]), p. 231.

12. Robert Nichols, *Theft Is Property! Dispossession and Critical Theory* (Durham, NC: Duke University Press, 2020), p. 8.

13. Ibid., p. 98.

14. Alexander G. Weheliye, *Habeas Viscus: Racializing Assemblages, Biopolitics, and Black Feminist Theories of the Human* (Durham, NC: Duke University Press, 2014), p. 3.

15. Saidiya V. Hartman, *Scenes of Subjection: Terror, Slavery, and Self-Making in Nineteenth-Century America* (New York: Oxford University Press, 1997), pp. 65–70.

16. Ibid., p. 62.

17. Cheryl I. Harris, "Whiteness as Property," *Harvard Law Review* 106, no. 8 (June 1993): 1721.

18. Ibid., 1780.

19. Mamdani, *Neither Settler nor Native*, p. 109.

20. Mamdani writes, "When it came time for judgment at Nuremberg, the Americans and other non-Germans who had supported the Reich politically and economically were not brought to account, and the US influence on Nazi decision-making was inadmissible at the court proceedings. This is a key mechanism by which denazification left Nazism itself intact. To put Nazism—as opposed to individual Nazis—on trial would have revealed that it was not just a German project but also an American one and indeed a global one; a complex of the nation-state and big business, working toward the aims inherent in themselves." Ibid, p. 108.

21. Foucault's *The Order of Things* is devoted to historicizing the concept of "Man" and ends with a famous fantasy of this figure's disappearance. Michel Foucault, *The Order of Things: An Archaeology of Human Sciences* (New York: Vintage Books, 1994) [originally published in French as *Les mots et les choses*, 1966].

22. Sylvia Wynter, "Unsettling the Coloniality of Being/Power/Truth/ Freedom: Towards the Human, After Man, Its Overrepresentation —An Argument," *CR: New Centennial Review* 3, no. 3 (Fall 2003): 266.

23. Ibid., 260.

24. Adrian Piper, "IV. Concretized Ideas I've Been Working Around" [January 1971], in Adrian Piper, *Out of Order, Out of Sight*, vol. 1, *Selected Writings in Meta-Art, 1968-1992* (Cambridge, MA: MIT Press, 1996), pp. 42–43.

25. F. R. Ankersmit, *Aesthetic Politics: Political Philosophy beyond Fact and Fiction* (Stanford, CA: Stanford University Press, 1996), p. 45.

26. Ibid., p. 49.

27. Ibid., p. 50.

28. Richard Shiff, *Cézanne and the End of Impressionism: A Study of the Theory, Technique, and Critical Evaluation of Modern Art* (Chicago: University of Chicago Press, 1984), p. 19. Shiff's assertion of a moment beyond subject/object distinction is very similar to the claim made by Yve-Alain Bois that what he calls Matisse's "arche-drawing" represents a collapse of the opposition between color and drawing:

"Just as 'arche-writing' is 'prior' to the hierarchization of speech and writing [for Jacques Derrida], and, being productive of difference itself, forms their common 'root' (which goes for all the hierarchical oppositions out of which western metaphysics is woven, notably the opposition between sign and meaning), so 'arche-drawing' would be 'prior' to the drawing/color opposition." See Yve-Alain Bois, "Matisse and 'Arche-Drawing,'" in *Painting as Model* (Cambridge, MA: MIT Press, 1990), p. 22.

29. Frank B. Wilderson III, *Red, White and Black: Cinema and the Structure of U.S. Antagonisms* (Durham, NC: Duke University Press, 2010), p. 18.

30. Ibid., p. 21.

31. See Orlando Patterson, *Slavery and Social Death: A Comparative Study* (Cambridge, MA: Harvard University Press, 1982). Patterson defines his understanding of natal alienation on pp. 5–14.

32. Quoted in Paul Greenhalgh, *Ephemeral Vistas: The Expositions Universelles, Great Exhibitions and World's Fairs, 1851–1939* (Manchester, UK: Manchester University Press, 2017), pp. 83–84.

33. Frantz Fanon, *Black Skin, White Masks*, trans. Richard Philcox (New York: Grove Press, 2008 [originally published in French as *Peau noire masques blancs*, 1952]), p. 95.

34. Ibid., p. 119.

35. On this exhibition, see: Shawn Michelle Smith, "'Looking at One's Self through the Eyes of Others': W.E.B. Du Bois's Photographs for the 1900 Paris Exposition," *African American Review* (Winter 2000), vol. 34 (4), pp. 581–99; Whitney Battle-Baptiste and Britt Russert, eds., *W.E.B. Du Bois's Data Portraits Visualizing Black America: The Color Line at the Turn of the Twentieth Century* (New York: Princeton Architectural Press, 2018); W.E.B. Du Bois, *Black Lives 1900: W.E.B. Du Bois at the Paris Exposition*, with an introduction by Jacqueline Francis and Stephen G. Hall (London: Redstone Press, 2019); and *A Small Nation of People: W.E.B. Du Bois and African American Portraits of Progress*, with essays by David Levering Lewis and Deborah Willis (Washington, DC: Library of Congress, 2003).

36. W. E. Burghardt Du Bois, "The American Negro at Paris," *American Review of Reviews*, November 1900, p. 577.

The Burden of Representation

1. In the 1967 essay "Fantasia of the Library," Foucault writes, "*Déjeuner sur l'Herbe* and *Olympia* were perhaps the first 'museum' paintings, the first paintings in European art that were less a response to the achievement of Giorgione, Raphael, and Velasquez than an acknowledgement (supported by this singular and obvious connection, using this legible reference to cloak its operation) of the new and substantial relationship of painting to itself, as a manifestation of the existence of museums and the particular reality and interdependence that paintings acquire in museums." Michel Foucault, *Language, Counter-Memory, Practice: Selected Essays and Interviews by Michel Foucault*, ed. and introduction by Donald F. Bouchard, trans. Donald F. Bouchard and Sherry Simon (Ithaca, NY: Cornell University Press, 1977), p. 92.

2. W.E.B. Du Bois, *The Souls of Black Folk*, in *W.E.B. Du Bois: Writings*, ed. Nathan Huggins (New York: Library of America, 1986) [originally published in 1903], p. 359.

3. For a history of this phenomenon, see Pascal Blanchard, Gilles Boëtsch, and Nanette Jacomijn Snoep, *Exhibitions: L'Invention du sauvage* (Paris: Musée du quai Branly, 2011).

4. See Kobena Mercer, "Black Art and the Burden of Representation," *Third Text* 4, iss. 10 (1990): 61–78.

5. Fred Moten speaks of the pictures of Emmett Till as follows: "So that mourning turns. So that the looker is in danger of slipping, not away, but into something less comfortable than horror—aesthetic judgment, denial, laughter, some out and unprecedented reflection, movement, murder, song. So that there is an inappropriable ecstatics that goes along with this aesthetics—one is taken out, like in screams, fainting, tongues dreams. . . . The refusal to neutralize the phonic substance of the photograph rewrites the time of the photograph, the time of the photograph of the dead." Fred Moten, *In the Break: The Aesthetics of the Black Radical Tradition* (Minneapolis: University of Minnesota Press, 2003), p. 201. For a reading of the duration of photographs, see also Campt, *Listening to Images*.

6. Audre Lorde, "Afterimages," in *The Collected Poems of Audre Lorde* (New York: W. W. Norton, 1997), pp. 342.

7. All quotes from Hannah Black's open letter to the curators of the Whitney Biennial, reprinted in full in Lorena Muñoz-Alonso, "Dana Schutz's Painting of Emmett Till at Whitney Biennial Sparks Protest," Artnet, March 21 2017, accessed June 14, 2021, https://news.artnet.com/art-world/dana-schutz-painting-emmett-till-whitney-biennial-protest-897929.

8. In her excellent overview and analysis of the Schutz affair, Aruna D'Souza draws attention to this issue in her conclusion in a way that addresses the relation between persons and things. In speaking of the backlash that met Black's call to destroy the painting, she writes: "In a sense, the open letter was designed to create such a reaction by putting the call for painting's destruction out front, laying bare once again the way that liberal culture seems consistently to value things over people." Aruna D'Souza, "Act 1: *Open Casket*, Whitney Biennial, 2017," in *Whitewalling: Art, Race & Protest in 3 Acts*, with artwork by Parker Bright and Pastiche Lumumba (New York: Badlands Unlimited, 2018), p. 58.

9. Muñoz-Alonso, "Dana Schutz's Painting of Emmett Till at Whitney Biennial Sparks Protest."

10. Andrew Goldstein, "Why Dana Schutz's Emmett Till Painting Must Stay: A Q & A with the Whitney Biennial's Christopher Lew," Artnet, March 30, 2017, accessed June 14, 2021, https://news.artnet.com/art-world/whitney-biennial-christopher-lew-dana-schutz-906557.

11. Ruth Feldstein, *Motherhood in Black and White* (Ithaca, NY: Cornell University Press, 2018), p. 102. Chapter 4 of Feldstein's book, "'I Wanted the Whole World to See': Constructions of Motherhood in the Death of Emmett Till," gives a close reading of Till-Mobley's precarity as a "good mother" under the conditions of white supremacy.

12. Aria Dean, "The Demand Remains," *New Inquiry*, March 28, 2017, accessed June 15, 2021, https://thenewinquiry.com/the-demand-remains/.

13. Christina Sharpe, author of *In the Wake: On Blackness and Being* (Durham, NC: Duke University Press, 2016), told an interviewer, "It was not mainstream media—or white media—that published those images. It was *Jet* magazine. And those images had nothing to do with white consciousness. They were for Black people, because *Jet*

was a Black publication. They weren't meant to create empathy or shame or awareness from white viewers. They were meant to speak to and to move a Black audience." Siddhartha Mitter, "'What Does It Mean to Be Black and Look at This?' A Scholar Reflects on the Dana Schutz Controversy," *Hyperallergic*, March 24, 2017, accessed August 24, 2021, https://hyperallergic.com/368012/what-does-it-mean-to-be-black-and-look-at-this-a-scholar-reflects-on-the-dana-schutz-controversy/.

14. Coco Fusco, "Censorship, Not the Painting, Must Go: On Dana Schutz's Image of Emmett Till," *Hyperallergic*, March 27, 2017, accessed June 17, 2021, https://hyperallergic.com/368290/censorship-not-the-painting-must-go-on-dana-schutzs-image-of-emmett-till/.

15. Goldstein, "Why Dana Schutz's Emmett Till Painting Must Stay."

16. Calvin Tomkins, "Troubling Pictures: Dana Schutz Painted a Real-Life Atrocity. She Knew It Was a Risk," *New Yorker*, April 10, 2017, p. 35.

17. Klaus Speidel, "Dana Schutz's 'Open Casket': A Controversy around a Painting as a Symptom of an Art World Malady," *Spike Art Magazine*, March 24, 2017, accessed June 17, 2021, https://www.spikeartmagazine.com/articles/dana-schutzs-open-casket-controversy-around-painting-symptom-art-world-malady.

18. Zadie Smith, "Getting In and Out: Who Own's Black Pain?" *Harper's Magazine*, June 30, 2017, accessed June 23, 2021, https://harpers.org/archive/2017/07/getting-in-and-out/.

Witness

1. Mamie Till-Mobley and Christopher Benson, *Death of Innocence: The Story of the Hate Crime That Changed America* (New York: One World, Random House, 2003), p. 101.

2. bell hooks, "Representing Whiteness in the Black Imagination," in Lawrence Grossberg, Cary Nelson, Paula Treichler, eds., *Cultural Studies* (New York: Routledge, 1992), p. 340.

3. "Lynching," *Crisis* 10, no. 2 (June 1915): 71, quoted in Leon F. Litwack, "Hellhounds," in James Allen et al., *Without Sanctuary: Lynching Photography in America* (Santa Fe, NM: Twin Palms, 2010), p. 11.

4. Mitter, "'What Does It Mean to Be Black and Look at This?'"

5. Tomkins, "Troubling Pictures," p. 30.

6. Adriana Cavarero, *Relating Narratives: Storytelling and Selfhood*, trans. and introduction by Paul A. Kottman (London: Routledge, 2000 [originally published in Italian as *Tu che mi guardi, tu che mi racconti*, 1997]), p. 13.

7. Hannah Arendt, "Isak Dinesen: 1885-1963," in *Men in Dark Times* (San Diego and New York: Harcourt Brace and Company, 1968), p. 105, quoted in Cavarero, *Relating Narratives*, p. 3.

8. Cavarero, *Relating Narratives*, p. 36.

The Object as Witness

1. For reasons that I hope I have made clear in the course of this book, I do not believe that there was a significant structural or epistemological break between modern art and postmodern/contemporary art. This belief is encapsulated in my assertion that modern art was always conceptual, that both modern and contemporary art belong to the episteme of possessive individualism that arose at the conjunction of modern democracy and capitalism.

2. Rowland cites this first section of the Thirteenth Amendment in the exhibition booklet for *91020000*. Accessed July 7, 2021, https://texts.artistsspace.org/uwcc1tpk.

3. Rowland explains in the exhibition booklet how he arrived at the show's title: "*91020000* is the customer number assigned to Artists Space upon registering with Corcraft; the market name for the New York State Department of Corrections and Community Supervision, Division of Industries."

4. For an account of how the readymade strategy has functioned under conditions of art's globalization, see my *Heritage and Debt*.

5. Rowland, exhibition booklet for *91020000*.

6. For an important account of how the archive of slavery has come down to us, in part, through financial records of the slave trade, see Ian Baucom, *Specters of the Atlantic: Finance Capital, Slavery and the Philosophy of History* (Durham, NC: Duke University Press, 2005).

7. For an indispensable account of Rowland's use of contracts and practice of renting works in this exhibition and elsewhere, see Eric

Golo Stone, "Legal Implications: Cameron Rowland's Rental Contract," *October* 164 (Spring 2018): 89–112.

8. Rowland's is by no means the only way of narrating incarceration and the disproportionate harm it causes to African Americans through art. I dwell on his strategy because it is so intimately tied to the politics of private property that are the central concern of *Art's Properties*. Another important approach is that of Nicole R. Fleetwood in her curatorial work, including the exhibition *Marking Time: Art in the Age of Mass Incarceration*, which took place at MoMA PS1 in New York in 2020–21, and her book, *Marking Time: Art in the Age of Mass Incarceration* (Cambridge, MA: Harvard University Press, 2020). Fleetwood's work is founded in years of research in prisons and with incarcerated and formerly incarcerated artists. Her project is one of acknowledging how incarcerated men and women recount their narratives of captivity in a wide range of genres and styles under the restraints of what she calls "carceral aesthetics." Carceral aesthetics encompasses three dimensions: "penal space," including "the sites in prison where incarcerated people create, such as structural workshops, hobby and crafts rooms, recreational areas, and sometimes alone in isolation cells" (38), but also the general architecture of constraint and surveillance; "penal time," which "encompasses the multiple temporalities that impact the lives of the incarcerated and their loved ones. It refers to sentencing guidelines but also significantly invokes how modern theories of penalty turn time into a mode of punishment" (39); and finally, "penal matter," referring to "the material conditions of imprisonment, which include extreme restrictions on what incarcerated people can possess" (42). Under these multiple restrictions, incarcerated artists have created a wide variety of projects that address—even redress—the central problem of what Fleetwood calls "carceral visuality": that it "makes incarcerated people both invisible and hyper visible, but also unseeing and unseen" (16). The incarcerated are hypervisible in their ubiquitous (mis)representation in popular culture, while their actual everyday reality is largely kept out of public view. Fleetwood demonstrates that making art in prison is a means of narrating the conditions of the incarcerated in the face of their marginalization both physically and in the spectacular visuality of popular culture. Crucial to these

aesthetic activities is the effect of creating community within the prison, as well as with un-incarcerated friends and relatives and through exhibitions like *Marking Time*, with a broader public.

Afterword

1. This is Weheliye's formulation. Weheliye, *Habeas Viscus*, p. 3.

Index

Image Credits

© MVRDV and Ossip van Duivenbode (fig. 1); Musée Carnavalet, Histoire de Paris (fig. 2); Generali Foundation Collection—Permanent Loan to the Museum der Moderne Salzburg, © Generali Foundation, Photographer: Rosemary Mayer (fig. 3); Bibliothèque historique de la Ville de Paris (fig. 4); Library of Congress Prints and Photographs Division, Washington, DC (fig. 5); © Benjamin Norman (fig. 6); © Johnson Publishing Company Archive, courtesy Ford Foundation, J. Paul Getty Trust, John D. and Catherine T. MacArthur Foundation, Andrew W. Mellon Foundation and Smithsonian Institution, © JET Media Group, LLC (fig. 7); ST-17600658, Chicago Sun-Times Collection, Chicago History Museum, © Sun-Times Media, LLC (fig. 8); Collection of the Smithsonian National Museum of African American History and Culture, © Estate of David C. Driskell, courtesy DC Moore Gallery, New York (fig. 9); © The artist and Maxwell Graham/ Essex Street, New York (figs. 10 and 11).